Leone Levi

Work and pay; or, Principles of industrial economy. Two courses of lectures delivered to working men in King's college, London

With report of the Committee of the British association on combinations of labourers and capitalists

Leone Levi

Work and pay; or, Principles of industrial economy. Two courses of lectures delivered to working men in King's college, London
With report of the Committee of the British association on combinations of labourers and capitalists

ISBN/EAN: 9783337229535

Printed in Europe, USA, Canada, Australia, Japan

Cover: Foto ©Suzi / pixelio.de

More available books at **www.hansebooks.com**

WORK AND PAY:

OR,

PRINCIPLES OF INDUSTRIAL ECONOMY.

Two Courses of Lectures delivered to Working Men

IN KING'S COLLEGE, LONDON.

WITH

REPORT OF THE COMMITTEE OF THE BRITISH ASSOCIATION
ON COMBINATIONS OF LABOURERS AND CAPITALISTS.

By LEONE LEVI, F.S.A., F.S.S.,

PROFESSOR OF THE PRINCIPLES OF COMMERCE AND COMMERCIAL LAW IN KING'S
COLLEGE, LONDON; DOCTOR OF POLITICAL ECONOMY; AND OF
LINCOLN'S INN, BARRISTER-AT-LAW.

STRAHAN AND CO., LIMITED,
34, PATERNOSTER ROW, LONDON.
1877.

TO

SAMUEL MORLEY, ESQ., M.P.

Dear Sir,—

These lectures are the outcome of the Bristol Meeting of the British Association, when the report of its Committee on Combinations of Capitalists and Labourers was read and discussed. And they owe their delivery to your earnest desire to have the important questions at issue between masters and men treated in a calm spirit and in an impartial manner. I do not lay claim to the enunciation of any new theories, or to any novelty in argument. What I have advanced is nothing more than what the well-established principles of political economy, recognised alike in their essentials by British and foreign economists, have taught us.

Your desire and mine is that the relations between capital and labour be placed on a sound and equitable basis, and I earnestly trust that the effort now made to bring the principles of economic science and the interests and aspirations of the working classes into direct contact and possible harmony may have a beneficial influence on the well-being of the people.

Believe me, dear Sir, yours very faithfully,

LEONE LEVI.

5, Crown Office Row, Temple,
March, 1877.

CONTENTS

LECTURE	PAGE
I. WORK AND WORKERS	1
II. THE DIVISION OF LABOUR AND THE WONDERS OF MACHINERY	17
III. USE OF CAPITAL IN INDUSTRY	33
IV. THE REWARD OF LABOUR	49
V. TRADE UNIONS	67
VI. STRIKES AND LOCKOUTS	85
VII. BUDGETS OF THE WORKING CLASSES	96
VIII. SAVINGS BANKS AND OTHER INVESTMENTS OF THE WORKING CLASSES	111

APPENDIX.

(A) COST OF LIVING IN 1839, 1849, 1859, 1875	129
(B) WAGES IN 1839, 1849, 1859, 1873	130
(C) BUDGETS OF THE WORKING CLASSES	131
(D) REPORT OF THE COMMITTEE OF THE BRITISH ASSOCIATION	137

I.

WORK AND WORKERS.

IF I venture to come before you, in this great centre of labour, to discuss some of those questions connected with "Work and Pay" which so often give occasion to quarrels and difficulties, it is in the full consciousness that the proper solution of economic problems depends not only on the right conception of abstract theories and principles, but on their being regarded side by side with the realities of life. I do not pretend to be a philosopher, but I would like to be a practical economist. If I am able to state to you what I consider the dictates of economic science on the questions before us, you may also be able to point out to me how such dictates are found to work in practical life. In any case, should I be unable to carry conviction into your mind, should you see reason to object to any principles I may lay before you, I hope you will not refuse giving due heed to the lessons and warnings of a science which is essentially connected with the progress and wealth of the nation.

It is cheering to know that we are all wanted in this wide world; that all of us have a purpose to accomplish, and that, if we have only the will to exercise them, our faculties need not lie dormant, or languish. To me, and to all of us, constituted as we are, it is a real pleasure to work. I delight in a tableful of papers. I do not sympathize with the sentiment, *dolce far niente;* I rather believe in the adage, "A mind at rest is a mind unblest." With our powers of thought and imagination, and with our capacity of invention, construction, and intercourse, we must be active in order to be happy. The use of such expressions as "condemned to labour," or the "task of labour," or the calling of labour of any kind "servile," whilst we enjoy full freedom of labour, betokens simple ignorance of its dignity and utility. Sometimes, indeed, we may be disappointed at the result of our labour. Occasionally, it may be, thorns and thistles spring where we expected luxuriant fruitfulness and beauty. But what then? The necessity to meet our daily wants, and even our failure to accomplish the object of our aspirations, often prove a salutary incentive to strengthen and refine the powers and faculties with which we are endowed. One thing is absolutely certain, that without labour nothing is produced. The sun, water, fire, wind, gravitation, magnetism, the vital forces of animals, the vegetative forces of the soil, the duration, resistance, and ductility of metals, whatever active or inert forces may exist, if left to themselves they will not exist for us, and will be quite indifferent to our happiness. That they may serve us, they must be turned to our service; that they may be able to produce, they must be directed in the work of production. Though they exist independently of us, as agents of production, they exist only by human industry.

> ". . . Nature lives by labour;
> Beast, bird, air, fire, the Heavens and rolling world,
> All live by action; nothing lives at rest,
> But death and ruin!" *

We often speak of the working classes as a distinct body of persons upon whom mainly fall the work and toil of life. What a blunder! We are all workers. Every one of us, from the Queen on the throne to the humblest of her subjects, has a place to fill and a work to do. Some are labouring in directing and administering the affairs of the State. They are the Ministers of State, the Governors of Colonies, the whole Civil

* Dyer.

Service. Some are engaged in extracting the fruit of the soil, in appropriating, adapting, converting, shaping matter to our convenience. They work the land. They are busy with animal and vegetable substances and minerals. Many are fulfilling various offices for man—curing diseases, teaching youth, preserving peace, defending right, punishing wrong, and in a thousand ways upholding the great structure of human society. Some work in the field, some in workshops, some in the mines, and some on the sea. Some labour with the hand, some with the head, and some with both. Yes, we are all workers. Strictly speaking, we may not be all producers of wealth; all labour being, economically speaking, unproductive which ends in immediate enjoyment without tending to any increase of permanent stock, or not having for its result a material product. Yet we can scarcely say that no labour is valuable which is not immediately employed in the production of material riches. The genius which enlightens, the religion which comforts, the justice which preserves, the sciences and arts which improve and charm our existence, are indirectly, if not in a direct manner, as truly productive as commerce, which affords us the enjoyment of the produce and labour of other countries; as agriculture, which extracts the fruit special to each soil; and as manufactures, which transform the raw produce of different countries into articles adapted to the taste and wants of the opulent, as well as of the masses of the people. Few, indeed, who truly fulfil the mission to which they are called, who labour in the sphere and condition in which they are placed, and who exercise the faculties and talents with which they are endowed, can be said to be unproductive in this great laboratory. The whole nation is practically working together as a great co-operative society, under the very best division of labour; all the more perfect since it is natural and spontaneous. Let us perform our part well, and we need not fear but our labour will be useful. Ashamed of working?—

> "Work, work! be not afraid,
> Look labour boldly in the face;
> Take up the hammer or the spade,
> And blush not for your humble place.
>
> There's glory in the shuttle's song,
> There's triumph in the anvil's stroke,
> There's merit in the grave and strong,
> Who dig the mine or fell the oak.
>
> The wind disturbs the sleeping lake,
> And bids it ripple pure and fresh,
> It moves the grain boughs till they make
> Grand music in their leafy mesh."

I have often wondered at the power of endurance of the human frame when engaged in some of the most arduous tasks of manual labour. It must be hard to be continually lifting enormous weights, to deal with such substances as iron and steel, to stand the heat of a fiery furnace, or to work for hours in the very bowels of the earth. But do not imagine that those who labour with the head have a much lighter work. The headache, the excited nerve, the sleepless eye, of the man of letters are as irksome and injurious to life as the undue exercise of our physical energies. An agricultural labourer, working in the open air with mind and heart perfectly at ease, has a greater expectancy of life than a solicitor or a physician. The distinction, moreover, between manual and intellectual labour is no longer so marked as it once was. It is ungenerous to assume that the manual labourer employs no skill, for what labour is there which does not need skill and judgment? What are the wonderful results of machinery, those exquisite examples of handicraft at our Kensington Museum, but so many monuments of the talent and dexterity of those who are engaged in so-called manual labour? Among the labouring classes there is a wonderful and endless variety of talent and skill. Between the Michael Angelos employed by a Bond Street goldsmith, and the common labourer employed in the East and West India Docks, the gradations are most numerous. We speak of a million of men engaged in agricultural work, of half a million in the building trade, of a third of a million employed in the textile manufacture, and of a third more in tailoring and shoemaking. But really these different descriptions of workmen divide themselves into as many classes as they have special skill and capacity. Together, they cultivate during the yea 47,000,000 acres of land, rear 32,000,000 sheep and 10,000,000 cattle, extract some £65,000,000 worth of minerals, produce goods for export to the extent of £200,000,000, and bring into existence ever so many commodities and utilities needed for the sustenance, comforts, and luxuries of the inhabitants of all countries. But to what extent each individual labourer assists in this work it would be difficult to say. I fear the difference is in many cases enormous.

It is well indeed to remember what are the conditions for the efficient discharge of duties in the work of production. To my mind, first and foremost amongst such conditions is energy, or the possession of a good strong will to work; for with indolence and carelessness no work is done, no wealth is produced. There must be steady and persevering labour, and an energetic and willing mind to overcome the difficulties which Nature presents. An impulsive and transient effort is not sufficient. How far it is true that six Englishmen can do as much work as eight Belgians or Frenchmen, I do not know; but to be able to do a certain amount of work, and to give oneself in earnest to do it, are two distinct things. There is such a thing, let it be remembered, as idling away our time whilst we profess to work, as laying 500 bricks in a day when 1000 might easily be laid, as giving five blows to strike a tree-nail when three ought to be sufficient. A day's work means a day of continuous, energetic work—a day in which as much work is done as can possibly be done, a day in which our powers and talents are employed in full active service, when the work is gone through thoroughly, speedily, earnestly. To pretend to be working when you are wasting your time in idle talk, is to defraud your master of the value of your service. To make a show of work is a very different thing from doing real work. Then there is another consideration. How many days in the year do you work? An Irishman's year used to be 200 days, instead of at least 300; for he had 52 Sundays, 52 market-days, a fair in each month, half a day a week for a funeral, and some 13 days in the year as saints'-days and birthdays. What a waste! "Alas for that workman who takes all the Mondays for pastime and idleness, who keeps fairs and wakes, or who deliberately neglects the work which a bountiful Providence set before him! Miserable is he who slumbers on in idleness. Miserable the workman who sleeps before the hour of his rest, or who sits down in the shadow whilst his brethren work in the sun."* There is enough of forced idleness and slack time in every occupation, without aggravating the evil by wilful neglect. "To live really," said Mr. Smiles, "is to act energetically. Life is a battle to be fought valiantly. Inspired by high and honourable resolve, a man must stand to his post, and die there, if need be. Like the old Danish hero, his determination should be to dare nobly, to will strongly, and never falter in the path of duty."

> "Let us go forth, and resolutely dare
> With sweat of brow to toil our little day;
> And if a tear fall on the task of care,
> Brush it not by!"

The national characteristics of each country are sure to be reflected in the work performed by its people. Her Majesty's Secretaries of Legation reported of the French that there is much instability in their manner of work; that the workmen are most competent when it suits their fancy to display their skill, but that, as a rule, they do not work steadily. Of the Germans, that their work is well performed, but that their chief fault is slowness and indifference as to time in completing their task. The quality

* Tynman.

of the work in Italy is not to be despised, but the workmen require a great amount of watching, their conscience not being at all sensitive. Of the Swiss, they say that, as a rule, they are competent for their work, and that they do take an interest in it. The work of the Dutch is sound and good, but it has not the polish and finish of the English. The Russians, the Secretary of Legation reports, seem utterly indifferent as to the quality of their labour. They take no pride in their work, and require the most constant supervision. The Turks perform their work roughly, rudely, and incompletely. The Argentines turn out a rough and unfinished work. And our friends in the United States have many short cuts for arriving at what may not be quite equal to the article turned out in the English workshop. Rare are the instances where absolute praise is awarded for energy, where it can be said with truth that the labourers do really take a pride in their work, and throw their character into it. What reports are the Secretaries of Foreign Legations in England sending out to their Governments as regards work in this country? Is there good foundation for the complaint of the deterioration of work in many branches of British labour? Nearly one hundred years ago, a German writer described the Englishman as the best workman in the world; for he worked so as to satisfy his own mind, and always gave his work that degree of perfection which he had learnt to appreciate and attain. As the Frenchman sought to enhance the value of his manufactures by all kinds of external ornament, so the Englishman sought to give his productions in exactitude, usefulness, and durability a less fleeting worth. Has this important encomium been forfeited? I do not think so, whatever may be said to the contrary. As a matter of fact it is seen in the cotton industry that an English labourer is able to superintend 74 spindles, whilst a German can at most superintend 35, a Russian 28, and a Frenchman 14. Physically and intellectually, the British workman is better than he ever was. I doubt, indeed, if he has a rival in his capacity for continuous exertion; and if there be reason to lament his disposition to obey with perfect discipline the mandates of such associations as undertake to protect his rights, we should not forget that it is that same disposition that best fits the British workman for taking his place in the modern organization of labour, where every human hand has work assigned, the value of which depends on the relation it bears to a great whole.

I am persuaded, however, that the exercise of energy in work depends in a great measure on the possession of strength and health; for it is impossible to work well unless we are in health and comfort. The body must be in full vigour, the vital energies must be elastic and fresh, the mental faculties must be quick and active, ere we can give ourselves to patient and persevering labour. Viewed in this aspect, every measure of sanitary reform has a direct economic value. How can you expect hard-working men and women where the very air is tainted by the most noxious gases? Liverpool, Manchester, and Salford, said Dr. Farr, are at the head of a mournful cohort of unhealthy districts which call aloud for healers. It is not the water, nor the food, nor the absence of food, nor the clothing that produce the mischief, but it is the heedless admixture of tallow-chandlery and slaughter-houses, and the vitiated atmosphere from the black outpourings from innumerable chimneys, that make the Manchester artisan pale, sallow, and unhealthy, and that make his children grow pale, thin, and listless. Many of our workmen, moreover, have to meet dangers peculiar to their occupations. They are liable to suffer from exposure to dust and other foreign substances, from exposure to noxious gases and heated and impure air, from mechanical concussions, from peculiar postures of body, and from excessive exertion. In the manufacture of artificial flowers or wall-paper with emerald-green, the workers are in danger of slow poisoning from arsenic. A dozen leaves from a lady's head-dress were found to contain ten grains of white arsenic. Those who have to do with phosphorous are exposed to its fumes, which produce jaw disease and bronchitic affections. The workers in lead are exposed to lead-poisoning, and those who work with mercury to mercurial poisoning; whilst builders, miners, fishermen, and seamen are in special danger of sudden death from falls, explosions, or storms. Domestic servants, always at home, comparatively at ease as respects the necessaries of life, may be supposed to have a good expectancy of life; yet carpenters and even metal-workers have better prospects of great age than they.

But, as I have just hinted, quite apart from dangers of this nature, other risks follow many of our workmen in their homes. Born, many of them, in the midst of comparative privations, living often in low, dingy, uncomfortable houses, how hard it is for them to maintain anything like freshness and vivacity. The rents of houses are certainly dear, and they often absorb a good portion of their weekly wages. Yet I apprehend that a comparatively high house-rent might be really a good investment, should it prevent, as it is sure to do, the slow deterioration of health, the lowered vitality of enjoyment, and the long series of evils arising from overcrowding. Room to breathe is wanted everywhere. Much good will, I hope, result from the recent Act for facilitating the improvement of the dwellings of the working classes; and good work is done in London by such associations as the Metropolitan Association for Improving the Dwellings of the Industrious Classes, the Improved Industrial Dwellings Company, and many other kindred societies. But all such efforts need the co-operation of the labouring classes themselves. How much an individual is justified in spending in house-rent it is difficult to say, circumstances varying so much. Ten per cent. of the income is, I believe, generally devoted to house-rent by the middle classes, whether by paying that proportion for a whole house, or by paying more and recovering a portion by sub-letting. But ten per cent. of the working man's wages, viz., three or four shillings a week on an income of thirty shillings to forty shillings, is hardly enough for sufficient accommodation for even a moderate family. Supposing, therefore, that twelve per cent. be required, or even fifteen per cent., better far to economise in other items of expenditure than to live in a house smaller than we require. In the economic management of a limited income the first thought should be an airy, wholesome, cheerful house—a real home for every inmate of the household. Need I say that there may be a house without a home? A house where father, mother, and children, some even of tender age, are absent from six in the morning to six or seven at night, can scarcely be called a home. Where mothers cease to nurse their children, and leave them to the tender mercies of servants, or deposit them at the Crèches, there must of necessity be a frightful mortality of children, a grievous degeneration of the race, and a total absence of moral education. And when, late in the evening, father, mother, and children meet together, more as strangers than as members of a common household, often in the only room they possess, empty and cheerless, what comfort can they expect? Alas! cleanliness in such a case is out of the question. The fire is out; the food is not ready; the children's clothing falls into rags; and, worse than all, father and brothers, disgusted, take refuge at the nearest public-house. I know nothing more essential, both in a social and economic aspect, than a happy home. "Home! If any of you working men have not got a home yet, resolve, and tell your wife of your good resolution, to get, to make it at almost any sacrifice. She will aid it all she can. Her step will be lighter and her hand will be busier all day, expecting the comfortable evening at home when you return. Household affairs will have been well attended to. A place for everything, and everything in its place, will, like some good genius, have made even an humble home the scene of neatness, arrangement, and taste. The table will be ready at the fireside; the loaf will be one of that order which says, by its appearance, You may cut and come again. The cups and saucers will be waiting for supplies. The kettle will be singing; and the children, happy with fresh air and exercise, will be smiling in their glad anticipation of that evening meal when father is at home, and of the pleasant reading afterwards."*

In matters of food and drink, I imagine, the British labourer is better off than the labourers of any other country. Meat is indeed dear, yet not dearer than in New York or Paris; whilst bread is decidedly cheaper, vegetables are abundant, and fish plentiful. And the people are doing full justice to such bounties. What a change in the quantities of foreign commodities consumed during the last thirty years! In 1844, there were 1½ lbs. of tea per head consumed in the United Kingdom; in 1875, 4·44 lbs. In 1844, ¾ lb. of foreign butter; in 1875, 4·92 lbs. In 1844, scarcely anything of foreign bacon and hams was consumed; in 1875, 8·26 lbs. per head. And, whilst the home production of wheat and flour is as large as ever, the consumption of wheat and flour of foreign countries increased from 17¾ lbs., in 1844, to 197 lbs. per head in 1875. How many who are now able to eat wheaten bread, were thirty years ago content with rye bread! and how many who never saw butcher meat from week to week, now enjoy it every day! Surely we may rejoice that by a wise legislation the door has been opened for the importation of the necessaries of life from every part of the globe; and that, as a result of the same and of other favourable circumstances, whereas the number of paupers, including indoor and outdoor, in 1849 was in the proportion of 5·73 per cent. of the population, in 1875 it was only 3·11 per cent. These are facts of unmistakable importance as regards the well-being of the people.

An important element in the maintenance of health is certainly the duration of labour; but how many hours a day a

* Helps.

workman may safely work in any industry without injury to his health must depend not only on the age and constitution of the worker, but on the kind of labour and the spirit with which the work is performed. I cannot say that, personally, I have much sympathy with any excessive indulgence for rest; for I am myself a great worker, having been often at my work sixteen or eighteen hours a day—not occasionally, but for weeks together; nor do I feel the slightest inconvenience from it. Yet it must be allowed that labour saved is not lost; and that unless we husband our strength, we stand a good risk of losing it altogether. I fully approve, therefore, of the legislation respecting labour in factories, which limits the number of hours of work to women and children. But let us not carry the matter too far. Remember, that even an hour a day extended over say 5,000,000 workpeople, working 300 days in the year, means a loss of 150,000,000 days a year. Doubtless such loss may be recovered by increased energy on the part of the workers, and by the introduction of improved 'machinery. As a matter of fact, at no time has England produced more than at present, notwithstanding the extension of the factory laws, and the widely diffused adoption of shorter hours. But is that a reason why we should indulge in idleness, beyond what is requisite for health and moderate enjoyment?

Hitherto I have dwelt on energy, physical strength, and health. It is necessary that I should add education as one of the very first conditions for the efficient discharge of duties in the work of production. Never was the saying, "Knowledge is power," more truly applicable than at present. Compare the value of skilled and unskilled labour. The demand for comparatively unskilled labour may be as great as ever, but the reward of skilled labour is certainly much greater. It is no new discovery, though it has, of late, acquired greater prominence, that in the work of production to sturdy will, patient endurance, and strong hands, we must add some knowledge of science, a cultivated mind, and a refined taste. Education and science must no longer remain the ornament and luxury of the few— they must become the necessary endowment of the many, if we will succeed in the great arena of industrial competition.

To what but to science does England owe her great achievements? Mechanical and chemical science have revolutionized the productive power of the country. It was but yesterday, comparatively, that in the coal beneath our feet we found a primary source of colour which makes England almost independent of the most costly dyewoods hitherto consumed in the ornamentation of the textile fabrics. Yet, with all our discoveries, and all our advantages, here we are but little in advance of other countries, and our only hope of maintaining our position depends on the success which we may yet attain in fathoming the inexhaustible secrets of Nature, on the increase in the number of patient yet ardent votaries of science, and still more, on the diffusion of education and scientific knowledge, among the great body of labourers. With the progress of civilization and refinement all over the world, it is no longer sufficient now to be able to produce what is cheap and plentiful, or objects adapted to the common wants of the masses. If England is to keep her place as the greatest manufacturing country in the world, we must endeavour, by the cultivation of the science of the perception of beauty, and by paying proper attention to the fine arts, to produce articles suitable to every state of civilization.

Much has been said, of late, on technical education, by which we understand the teaching of those sciences which are useful in industrial pursuits. Is it not a sound principle that the designer should know something of drawing, the dyer something of chemistry, the miner of geology and mineralogy? The chairmaker, the tailor, the bootmaker, the hatter, the coachmaker, and even the pastrycook, all require some knowledge of form. All honour then to the London

School Board for introducing drawing in their scheme of Elementary Education. How few, indeed, are at all acquainted with the scientific principles of their labour. An order comes for cloth of a particular shade of colour. How few can tell, beforehand, precisely, what manipulation will give it to a nicety! And if there be one in an establishment endowed with such knowledge, probably because he stumbled into it, he is deemed the possessor of a great mystery. But why should it be so? Science need neither be a mystery nor a monopoly. Its pages are open to all, and let us not think that its meaning is hid or incomprehensible to the common understanding. With the simplicity of language ordinarily used, and the constant appeal to real facts by visible demonstrations and illustrations, the acquisition of scientific knowledge has been rendered wonderfully easy.

Apart from intellectual powers, however, I own great partiality for the moral. It seems to me that we must elevate, not the mind only, but the taste and affections of the people, if we wish to realize true progress. With such huge conglomerations of people as we have in this metropolis and in our manufacturing towns, quite away from the beauties of nature, we do need museums and galleries to educate the sense of the beautiful. What a power on our imagination have the common prints and representations which adorn our walls! What an effect the ornaments which cover our mantelpieces! Nor should we forget that more important even than the cultivation of the taste and the affections is the possession of good morals and simple piety. To secure a good reward, the labourer must not only have a good physical frame, and a proper aptitude for labour, but those qualities which create confidence and animate trust. Unless a labourer is worthy of confidence, it is impossible that he can be regularly employed. And what is it that creates confidence? Sober and steady conduct, truthfulness and purity of character, conscientiousness and strict regard to duty; in short, an abiding sense of the responsibility of our calling.

The requisites of production, John Stuart Mill said, are two—labour and appropriate natural objects. Certain lands are more favoured than others in natural productiveness. The climate has great influence in promoting vegetation, and in making the people hearty and robust. Numerous external influences, physical, economical, political, and social, determine more or less the success of labour. Taking it all in all, England is highly favoured as a field of human labour. Geographically, she is splendidly situated, on all sides open to communication with all the world. Her climate is most temperate. Coal and iron are sources of immense wealth. Her manufacturing industry is wonderfully developed. The commercial spirit of her people quite boundless. Her political organization, based on personal freedom to move, to speak, to meet, well nigh perfect. Her economical policy is immensely superior to that of almost any other nation. Can we wonder that her people are tranquil, that the Queen reigns supreme in the heart of the nation, and that wealth is increasing at an enormous ratio?

Where can you find a better field of labour than in England? Go to France, and you have no freedom of action and a constant dread of revolution. Go to Russia, and you meet despotism all rampant. Go to the United States, and you find that better wages are scarcely equivalent to the higher cost of living. Go to any of the British Colonies, and you must be prepared to work harder far than you are doing in this country, and to bid adieu to every association and to all the pleasures of civilized life. Nowhere, indeed, is labour more appreciated, nay, I might say more ennobled, than in this country, and nowhere is an ampler field afforded for its application.

But if labour is honoured, is the labourer receiving due consideration? Are his trials and difficulties taken into account? Are his wants as a man and a citizen properly recognised?

Alas! I fear not. On the contrary, there is far too ready a disposition to regard the labourers as a class as ignorant, wasteful, drunken, idle, and criminal. But where is the evidence for such a charge? In the number signing the marriage register with marks there is a vast improvement. The Savings-banks and Building Societies testify that the labouring classes have saved large sums in recent years. The yearly amount of production in the kingdom tells us that they have not been altogether idle; and if they drink more, or it may be are more amenable to its consequences than they formerly were, probably through better police administration, of crime, especially of the heavier character, they are certainly less guilty. They might be better, and so we all should be. But let us not indulge in sweeping condemnations of whole classes of the people. They are not true, and their effect is most injurious.

In the new organization of labour incident to production on a large scale, there is abundant scope for the display, by both masters and men, of those qualities which are essential for the maintenance of peace and concord. Let the master recognise, fully and unreservedly, the free position of the workman, and his absolute right to improve his condition. Let him see that labour be carried on under conditions, as favourable as possible, to the preservation of human health and vigour. Let him promote, as far as in him lies, provident habits and intellectual improvement among his labourers. Let him manifest a personal sympathetic interest in their behalf. Let the master do all this, and we shall also witness among workmen an increasing earnestness and energy in the execution of their work, a greater interest in the success of production, and a better disposition to apply all their forces, physical, intellectual, and moral, towards the surmounting of those obstacles which hinder and retard the economic progress of the nation.

II.

THE DIVISION OF LABOUR AND THE WONDERS OF MACHINERY.

WITHIN this century, within the recollection of many living among us, one of the greatest of economic revolutions has taken place, the consequence of which has far exceeded any human expectation. It is the substitute of collective for individual labour, of factory for home industry, and of mechanical for human labour. Time was when the weaver was both the capitalist and the labourer; when the linen weaver cultivated the flax, heckled it, spun it into yarn, wove it, and sold the web at the linen market. There was no division of labour in those days. The producer gloried in his independence. He was his own master. He did all the work himself. But production proceeded slowly in that fashion. And so the capitalist came to the rescue by supplying the weaver with the material, and paying him a given sum on the delivery of a given quantity of finished cloth. As yet, the loom belonged to the weaver; and if he had no loom of his own, he worked at a loom belonging to some other weaver, in which case he was the journeyman, and the weaver at whose loom he worked was the master weaver. But, in time, the loom itself was supplied by the capitalist or manufacturer; and then the journeyman, free from the master weaver, came into direct relation with the manufacturer. This is the system of home industry which existed in this country for a considerable time, certainly till as late as the end of the last century. And this is the system which obtains to a considerable extent in Russia at the present time. Employed in the actual work of agriculture only a portion of the year, the Russian farmer spends the remainder in weaving and bleaching.

The home system of industry has been passing away so rapidly from this country that we are apt to connect all manufacture with the machinery and steam power in use in the Lancashire cotton industry. But it is not so. And I venture to say that by far the largest amount of production in the north of Europe, in Asia, and Africa, and largely in America also, consists of home-made goods, which, though dearer in price, are in the end cheaper far than the trashy prints, and some of the highly-sized calicoes and other inferior descriptions of Manchester goods. The battle of the hand-loom against the power-loom, of home industry against factory labour, is not yet quite ended, for in not a few industries, especially in Nottingham and Leicester, hand-loom weavers are numerous. But of the final issue of the conflict who can doubt? In truth, young men do not take to the old and almost effete system. What remains of it is carried on by old people, and for those descriptions of labour only where the hand can work with more dexterity than the machine itself. But how soon is machinery overtaking every obstacle! And what a change has taken place in the divorcement of manufacture from agriculture, in the creation of great cities of labour, in the mode of producing on a large scale, in the division of labour, and the introduction of machinery!

From the moment the manufacturing system acquired a sufficient importance to stand by itself, from the moment the requirements of manufacture necessitated concurrence and cooperation in the various pursuits necessary for the same, the manufacturers were compelled to emigrate from the farmhouse and the sequestered village, and to constitute themselves into distinct communities. Both industries are indeed interdependent. Agriculture gains from the existence of a thriving manufacturing industry, and is the better for its products. Manufactures depend upon a prosperous agriculture for a suficiency of food and provision. But the two industries are not capable of being prosecuted in like manner. Agriculture does not admit of the same concentration of labour, of the same division of employment, and of the same constancy of labour. Even steam-power can only be employed in agriculture under less advantageous circumstances than in manufactures. The experience of every nation abundantly proves that the more absolute is the separation between the two industries, the better each may be developed in its own manner and fashion. Would, indeed, that the agricultural could copy a little more from the manufacturing industry than it appears to be doing! How much it has to learn in dealing with diversities of soil, in the reclamation of waste lands, in the introduction of machines and implements of husbandry, in the use of manure, and above all in the economy of labour and the application of scientific principles in the management of farms! Some writers used to distinguish agriculture from industry, the one being intent upon the extraction of produce from the soil, the other upon the shaping, converting, or manufacturing what nature supplies. But it is not so. Agriculture and manufactures are both industries requiring alike labour, skill, capital. In England, the divorce is indeed complete; but they had better look keenly to one another, and each draw from the other the lessons which it needs.

Look at Lancashire, the first county which inaugurated the great change. See how coal and iron have superseded turf and corn. Behold those illumined factories, with more windows than in Italian palaces, and smoking chimneys taller than Egyptian obelisks. Everywhere you find monuments of indomitable energy. All you see indicates the march of modern progress. Enter for a moment one of those numerous factories, behold the ranks of thousands of operatives all steadily working, behold how every minute of time, every yard of space, every practised eye, every dexterous finger, every active mind, is at high-pressure service. There are no lumber attics nor lumber cellars; everything seems cut out for the work, and the work for it. And what can be more wonderful than those factories for the manufacture of machines? Listen to the deafening din. What power has mind over matter! What metamorphoses can human industry perform! One hundred years ago, Manchester had only 1,600 inhabitants. Now, with Salford, she has 500,000. Three hundred years ago, Liverpool was only a fishing hamlet, with 138 inhabitants; now she has 527,000. Whilst Westmoreland, a purely agricultural county, has 7·71 acres to one person, Lancashire has only 0·43 acres to one person. In 1861, the town population of England was in the proportion of twenty-four per cent. of the whole. In 1871, her town population had increased to such an extent that it constituted fifty-six per cent. of the whole. The very meaning of the word town has changed. Whilst in olden times it meant a tract of land enjoyed by a community, though there might not be a single house in it; in modern times it has come to signify a place with a multitude of houses, built side by side, and standing in streets, rows, or lanes, all as like one another as possible,—the very personation of the Coketown of the inimitable Dickens.

Shall we lament the change from the primitive industrial organization of former days to the complex, and, in many ways, the artificial combination of the present time? Is England the better or the worse for the change? Have the working classes been injured or benefited by it? Could we return to the agricultural system if we would? And would we return to it if we could? Compare the state of England a hundred years ago and now, by any test you please, socially, politically, and morally, in education, wealth, power, population, agriculture, and manufactures. Nothing has been stationary. On every side we note change, progress, improvement. There are evils connected with the agglomeration of many people within fixed boundaries, for where ignorance, vice, crime, exists, oh how contagious it becomes! And yet, if you compare the moral condition of the agricultural and manufacturing districts, you will find that the latter are by no means inferior to the former, for if there is an army of evil-doers in our great cities, there are also many regiments of those who do well. Call the present organization of labour artificial, capitalistic, or by any title you please, yet the fact remains that not only is it the inevitable result of science, civilization, and economic progress, and therefore it is of no use whatever grumbling about it, but it is on the whole beneficial to the well-being of the people, an element of strength and power to the nation at large.

Steam, whose power dwarfs the fabled feats of Grecian prodigy, has not only torn asunder the manufacturing from the agricultural industry, but has centred industrial labour within large buildings and great factories. When human force was the only motive power, work could as advantageously be performed in the solitary chamber as in great centres of population; but when a force greater than human was discovered, which far exceeded the energies of any single individual, which needed no rest, which could be transported anywhere, and which could be regulated at discretion,—isolated working gave place to factory labour, and production on a small scale was immediately superseded by production on a large scale. Of course, factory labour has its own evils,—but what human system is free from them? With a motive power at hand capable of continuing without intermission, the temptation was too strong to use human labour as unsparingly. The comparatively light labour required to assist the machinery, prompted the employment of women and children; and their strength, by too long hours of employment, was taxed beyond measure. And so the Legislature had to interfere, in the way of fixing the number of hours that women and children should be allowed to work, of taking care that the education of such children shall not be altogether neglected, of compelling proper precautions against accidents from machinery, of providing for the health of the workers, and of securing by the right of inspection scrupulous compliance with the prescribed regulations. And thankful we may be that the provisions of such laws have been extended and strengthened, for we do need the protection of the law against abuse of power, whether by masters or by men. Apart, however, from such abuses which the law has set itself to rectify, there is a great principle involved in the present system of producing on a large scale of very wide reach and application. Do we not see large farms, large shops, large joint-stock companies, and large enterprises, fast superseding small farms, small shops, small partnerships, and small enterprises? And why? Simply because the expense of management and the labour of administration do not increase in proportion to the extension of the undertaking; because expensive machinery may be more advantageously employed; and because greater economy of power and administration is thereby obtained. In a large factory, moreover, the master can exercise more supervision of labour, can have more command over the detail of the work. And the result is more production, more wealth. The more united the forces, the greater the momentum.

And what shall I say of the division of labour, which production on a large scale permits? Adam Smith has well noted the increase of dexterity in every particular workman, the saving of time spent in passing from one species of work to another, and the happy contrivances for facilitating and abridging labour which such division of labour suggests and permits. Nothing, indeed, is more natural, and yet nothing is more wonderful in the present organization of labour, than the symmetry of its apportionment; the careful regard to the adaptation of the work to the worker. But little consideration suffices to convince us that the surest way to acquire a thorough knowledge of anything is to concentrate our thoughts, and to devote our energies almost exclusively upon the one thing before us. No science could be cultivated with any hope of success, were it not that special men give themselves to the innumerable researches which are required for their development. The physician, the chemist, the botanist, the mineralogist, the astronomer, each takes upon himself the study of special phenomena in nature. Sir David Brewster made optics his special study; Professor Owen devoted himself to fossils; Professor Liebig to organic chemistry; Professor Tyndal to light; Professor Huxley to physiology. Mr. Glaisher made his experiments on balloon ascents; Dr. Carpenter made observations on oceanic circulation. The principle of the division of labour with a view to the greater concentration of mental energies is of wide application, and, wherever applied, it of necessity leads to the greater efficiency and economy of labour. How natural the division of labour between agriculture, manufacture, and commerce! How consonant with the laws of nature the preference given in different countries to special industries! What is international commerce but the result of an extended division of labour? Of course the division of labour is limited by the power of exchange. One may confine himself to one specific branch of industry which may satisfy one kind of wants only, provided on the one hand he can find purchasers enough of that commodity as to render it worth his while producing nothing else, and provided also there are others ready to satisfy all the other wants. An extended division of labour demands a large and varied consumption. In little villages where the consumption of groceries is limited, the grocer is also the haberdasher, the stationer, the innkeeper. In London we have shops for certain specific classes of articles, and no more. But wherever the division of labour can be advantageously adopted, it is certain to be attended with advantage, at least in an economic aspect. And yet, that too has its evil, for it has certainly a tendency to concentrate the mind too consecutively to one operation, and it may have the effect of weakening a man's power, and make him become a mere machine. What fertility of invention, what independence of thought can you expect from a man who is required to do but one thing—say, to watch a pair of wheels, or to walk three steps forward and three steps backwards—throughout his lifetime? He will doubtless do that work more perfectly, more quickly, more economically, but the monotony and the sameness of the operation, and the want of excitement attending it, are sure to take away any spirit he might have.

Alas! nothing pleases us. Undivided work is very unproductive, too divided work is prejudicial to the human understanding. I am not ignorant of, and we cannot ignore or deny, the evils of the present organization of industry; but is it of any use to complain of them? Let us the rather strive to neutralize what is prejudicial, and set into motion remedies and influences which shall bring good out of evil. Let the church and the school be active in their work of moral and intellectual instruction. Let science and philanthropy devise good workable plans for the well-being of the masses of people huddled together in places unfit for human habitation. And if the family circle has still to be broken by the employment of women and children in factories, let us at least do our utmost to check vice, waste, luxury, extravagance, betting, gambling, drunkenness, and the license and wretchedness which meet us on every side—the result, to a large extent, of a vicious social system.

If it is to Watt and his wonderful engine that we owe the use of the new motive power, steam, it is to Arkwright, Hargreaves, Crompton, and many more illustrious inventors and discoverers, that we owe our machines and instruments for regulating the action of force. There is an intimate relation between the division of labour and machinery. If, on the one hand, it is the steam engine and machinery that have rendered division of labour possible, it is to the division of labour that we owe the large increase of machinery. The change wrought by machinery is something wonderful. A woman habituated to knit can make 80 stitches a minute. By the use of the circular loom, she can now make 480,000 stitches a minute, showing an increase of 6,000 times the quantity. To make by hand all the yarn spun in England in one year, by the use of the self-acting mule, carrying 1,000 spindles, viz., 1,000 threads at the time, we would require 100,000,000 of men. I have just spoken of knitting; but see what is done by the sewing machine. To make a shirt by the hand it takes at least fourteen hours; by the machine, less than two hours. A pair of trousers cannot be done by the hand in less than five hours; by the machine it may be done in one. A woman's chemise, which by the hand would take ten hours and a half, may be completed by the machine—ay, ornamented—in one hour. This is indeed the era of machines. We have the calculating machine and the electric machine. Hats are made by machinery, and so are opera-glasses. There is a machine to mould the mortar, a machine to make cigarettes, and a machine to make neck cravats. There are machines for measuring the wind, the evaporation, and the rain; machines for measuring the intensity and velocity of light; an instrument for measuring the interval between the appearance of the flash and the arrival of the sound; an instrument for measuring the pressure of the atmosphere, and an instrument for measuring the ten-thousandth part of an inch. The machine is simple when it transmits force in a direct manner; it is composite when it is composed of so many organs all combined and acting together in the transmission of force. But whether simple or complex, in whatever form or description, as a machine, an instrument, or a tool, their uniform tendency has been to take from the human hand some of the most drudgery work, to produce largely, to bring within the reach of the lowest classes many articles which were once rarities and luxuries. Machinery has lightened human labour of the most irksome tasks, and opened up to man the widest field for the exercise of his intellectual faculties. At one time it was muscular force that performed most of our work. Now, it is art, it is design, it is intellect. It is labour just the same, it is true, but it is nobler, higher, and more befitting our place and destinies, more in keeping with our aspirations and ambition. Only let workmen have sufficient dexterity in passing from one kind of labour to another, and the introduction of machinery is certain to prove a blessing, not a curse. But, alas! it is that capacity that is sometimes wanting.

Time was when inventions were the products of simple vagaries, or freaks of the imagination, of ignorant pretenders or mere charlatans. How to make a wheel turn by itself, and to get at perpetual motion; how to clean and keep bright the skin and flesh so as to preserve it in its perfect state; how to make upon the Thames a floating garden of pleasure, with trees, flowers, and fountains, and all in the midst of the stream where it is most rapid;—these were secrets and inventions of former days which contributed but little to the well-being of the people. Happily, the inventions, machines, and instruments of the present day are of a more utilitarian and sober caste, and they have immensely augmented, not only the wealth, but the comfort and the intelligence of the whole nation—ay, of the whole world. And who are the inventors? In many cases our working men themselves, and, strange to say, those very men who have to perform daily the same monotonous work, to repeat over and over again the operation of the same single member of a complicated whole. Yes, our working men, our artizans, are often able to suggest improvements in manufacture, and short cuts in workmanship, which economise labour, and are of immense value to the producers. Would that they were justly rewarded! A working man who has brain enough to invent a new article, or to use a new process, has a full right to the fruits of his labour, and to be rewarded for the product of his brain; and I am glad to know that sometimes, though not always, they do get the benefit of their inventions, either in an increased salary, or in a portion of the profits. Do not imagine, however, that the profits of an invention can go to any considerable extent into the pockets of the inventor, for the success of the invention depends often less on the fact of the invention itself, than on the appliances, energy, and capital employed in carrying it into practice. I should be glad if the cost of a patent were greatly reduced, in order to enable our working men to patent inventions for themselves even before they communicate them to their own employers; but oh how often the most sanguine hopes are placed on worthless inventions, how soon they are superseded, how often they prove more costly than they are worth! On the whole, the profession of an inventor is a profitless one, and it is this among other things that has more than once suggested the expediency of abolishing the Patent Laws altogether.

That machinery has immensely benefited production, and that it has placed a new engine of success in the hands of the producer, is beyond doubt, for though still depending upon labour, the machine enables the producer to spare a great number of labourers, whilst it immensely economises the cost of production. Once let him have a machine that will do the work of a thousand men, with only ten persons attending to it, and he is in a position to distance far any other manufacturer who wholly depends on human labour. How often indeed a persistence on the part of the labourer in asking higher wages than the business could afford, or demands of conditions of labour incompatible with its success, or the refusal to perform certain acts, or to allow other labourers to be introduced for their performance, have driven our manufacturers to introduce machinery!

But how has machinery affected the working classes? An inventor once proposed to Colbert, the great minister of Louis XIV. of France, a machine which would do the work of ten men. "I am anxious," said the minister, "that men should be able to live honestly by their work, and you propose to me to take the work out of their hands. Take the invention, if you please, somewhere else." Statesmen are often as ignorant of economic questions as the least among us, and just as when railways were projected all manner of apprehensions were entertained lest horses, cattle, and carriages should cease to be required, so when machines were introduced into any branch of industry, the first thought was, Well, labourers will no longer be wanted in it. But has it been so? Calculate the number employed in the occupation of transport and conveyance before and since the adoption of the railway system,—the number employed in the cotton manufacture, or any other textile industry, before and since the introduction of machinery,—the number employed in printing, copying, and publishing, before and since the invention of the printing machine. The first introduction of machinery may indeed displace and diminish for a while the employment of labour, may perchance take labour out of the hands of persons otherwise not able to take another employment, and create the need of another class of labourers altogether; but if it has taken labour from ten persons, it has provided labour for a thousand. How does it work? A yard of calico made by hand costs two shillings, made by machinery it may cost fourpence. At two shillings a yard, few buy it; at fourpence a yard, multitudes are glad to avail themselves of it. Cheapness promotes consumption: the article which hitherto was used by the higher classes only, is now to be seen in the hand of the labouring classes as well. As the demand increases, so production increases, and to such an extent, that although the number of labourers now employed in the production of calico may be immensely less in proportion to a given quantity of calico, the total number required for the millions of yards now used greatly exceeds the number engaged when the whole work was performed without any aid of machinery. And so as regards wages. Doubtless a manufacturer who has to pay for the use of an invention and for the cost and maintenance of the machinery, and who needs only a few labourers able to perform some mechanical act, might be tempted to take advantage of his position and to offer less wages. But if the cost of production and the maintenance of the machinery are more than replaced by the profits arising from increasing production, will not a large portion of those profits, in one way or another, fall on the labouring classes? And if to work the machinery, in the production of immensely larger quantities, the manufacturer requires more labourers than ever he did in the palmy days of hand labour, where will be his greater independence? No, no! Machinery may have decreased, in some cases, the *rates* of wages, but it has in all cases increased the total earnings of the labouring classes. It may have taken labour out of some, impoverished a few, done injury here and there, but it has given more labour to the community at large, and has added immensely to the resources of the artisans and labouring classes all the world over. M. Bastiat, in his excellent work on "What is Seen and What is not Seen in Political Economy," illustrated the operation of machinery on human labour in his usual spirited manner. "Jacque Bonhomme," he said, "had two francs, which he was in the habit of paying to two workmen whom he employed. Suddenly, however, having found out the means of abridging the work by half, he discharged one workman, and so saved one franc. Upon this, the ignorant is ready to exclaim, 'See how misery follows civilization! See how fatal is freedom to equality! The human mind has made a conquest, and immediately a workman falls into pauperism. Even if Jacque Bonhomme should continue to employ the two workmen, he will only give them half a franc each, for they will compete one with another, and they will offer their labour for half the money.' But it is not so, since both the premises and the conclusions are false. Behind the half of this phenomenon which is seen, there is another half which is not seen; for what does Jacque Bonhomme do with the other franc, which he saved? He employs it in another work, and whilst the same work is done for one franc by one workman which formerly required two to do it, extra work is done with the other franc, which employs the other also. The two workmen are as much employed as ever, but double work is done, and so the invention has procured a gratuitous benefit."

The introduction of machinery should never be used as a threat against the demands of labourers. It is *mean* to resort to such an expedient in order to frighten the labourers to acquiesce in the conditions offered. But remember, machinery is of great utility to production, and manufacturers may be compelled to introduce it for the salvation, possibly, of the whole industry. See what is taking place now in the watch manufacture of Switzerland. Hitherto watchmaking at Geneva has been almost entirely a hand-work industry. But Switzerland stands in danger of losing the industry altogether, since Germany and America have learnt to make watches and clocks by machinery. There is a certain protection, after all, against the sudden introduction of machinery in the fact that it is very costly, that it requires great capital, that manufacturers are very unwilling to alter their usual course of business, and that, in reality, in some industries the hand has some advantage over the machine, though machinery is now becoming so perfect and automatic that it is impossible to say what it cannot accomplish. It has been complained that the use of machinery often leads to over-production, and to gluts of merchandize, which redounds against the well-being of the masses especially by alternations of great activity and great depression. But a large production of articles of general use is always attended by increasing cheapness, and increasing cheapness most assuredly leads to an enlarged demand, which soon absorbs any surplus production.

Machine and tool making has become an important industry. In 1851 it employed in England and Wales 48,000 persons; in 1861, 117,000; and in 1871, 175,000. In 1851 our exports of steam engines, and other kinds, amounted to £1,168,000; in 1875, to £4,213,000. We export engines and machinery to every part of the world. Any one is now at liberty to order from the British workshop the most complex and the finest piece of machinery that can possibly be invented. It may be said, What folly it is to injure ourselves by enabling foreign manufacturers to obtain an advantage which is exclusively our own! True, England has superior facilities for the manufacture of machinery in her abundance of coal and iron, but the power of inventiveness is not confined within the British shores. In 1824, the Americans were considered as thirty years behind England, and France was the only country which could be said to rival England in the making of machinery. Since then, however, and for many years past, foreign countries have made wonderful progress. As well attempt to shut up all the avenues of science and knowledge as to secrete from public gaze the discoveries and inventions which benefit industry and manufacture.

It is well to realize that many of the primary conditions necessary to the development of manufacturing industry are no longer exclusively enjoyed by any country, and it would be folly for the British manufacturer to remain content and tranquil, as if he needed to dread no competition, and as if he could be sure to continue to enjoy the practical monopoly of the markets of the world. Greater command over capital, the possession of mineral resources almost boundless in extent and productiveness, greater commercial sagacity and power of enterprise, have hitherto kept and may yet keep Britain on a position of eminence above all her competitors; but in every one of these elements, France, Germany, Switzerland, and the United States are striving to advance; and with the most powerful machinery within the reach of every one, who can say how soon, from eager competitors, they may become formidable rivals? It would be a great mistake indeed on the part of our manufacturers to imagine that their only hope to preserve their supremacy rests in their being able to keep the wages of labour low. I have no faith in any plan which begins by starving the labourer. The essentials of real progress must ever consist in increasing power of production, in greater adaptiveness of our manufactures to the wants of the masses of the people at home and abroad, and in greater skill and advancement in the arts and sciences. Emulate other nations in their efforts to combine beauty with usefulness, elegance with solidity. Let nothing discourage the investment of capital in industry. Furbish your intellect to achieve greater wonders than were ever yet imagined. Let Capital and Labour march hand in hand, and England need not fear being outdone, however keen the contest, however close the issue.

III.

USE OF CAPITAL IN INDUSTRY.

ON the sea-coast of Sicily there was once a wild, lawless, gigantic race, who, with one eye in the middle of their forehead, but with strong hands, were constantly employed in forging thunderbolts for Jupiter. And in this island of Britain, there are many sons of the sturdy Saxon race who, with two eyes and both wide open, are constantly forging capital, not for Jupiter, but for the whole world. A disposition to labour, to save, and to accumulate; a growing conviction that wealth is power, whatever knowledge may be; a keen relish of the comforts of life, which wealth to a large extent provides; a decided aptitude for commerce, industry, and enterprise; confidence in the public institutions of the country; and a firm reliance on the impartial administration of justice,—these, together with those wonderful inventions and discoveries which have so enlarged the range and utility of human labour, have rendered Britain the great storehouse of capital, and at this moment borrowers from every nation are for ever coming to this modern Egypt, to buy capital of the living Josephs,—the Bank of England, the Rothschilds, the Barings, and many others who keep the keys of the coveted granary. An enviable position this for England to occupy. The taunt of contempt once expressed by the title *La Nation Boutiquière* (the shop-keeping nation), only betokens the sentiment of jealousy which

France once felt for this new power in the hands of England. But if England has got riches, it is because she has been industrious. If the broad acres of old England have become more luxurious and productive, if her mineral stores have become a source of perennial wealth, if her cities are full of people, and her manufacturing industry has become the wonder of all nations, it is simply because English labour and English perseverance have combated valorously with the obstacles presented by nature. What is the ocean to the daring British mariner? Boldly to the depths of the earth the British miner will venture, fearing nothing. Nature's inexhaustible riches and powers have all along animated the British discoverer to make unknown sacrifices. And so the British have thriven.

We might suppose that by this time every country would have become rich. With an old civilization, an immense population, untold resources, and varied opportunities, what is it that hindered the accumulation of wealth, and kept nearly every state in a condition of poverty? Alas! the work of destruction has been even more effective than the work of production. The warlike policy of the Roman Empire was not favourable to the production of wealth. In the Middle Ages, whatever was achieved by the thriving cities was more than destroyed by the injurious influence of feudalism and barbarism. Insecurity of person and property discouraged accumulation. Monopoly diverted the streams of wealth into narrow channels. Vicious fiscal systems often corroded the very sources of wealth. The Thirty Years' War, the Seven Years' War, and the French War, brought desolation into every home, and destroyed, not only all that had theretofore been produced, but even the produce of years to come. Can we wonder that under such circumstances but little or nothing was accumulated? Cast a glance beyond Europe. In Asia there has been much hoarding of wealth, but no accumulation and no workable capital. India has been rather the absorbent than the producer of capital. Africa is as yet destitute both of wealth and capital. And America, the land of promise for capital, is still, comparatively speaking, a new country, where the means of investment are always greater than the available resources for the same. There is no end of openings all over the world for the disposal of British capital; and for the interest of the great mass of our population we may well desire that, whatever the competition, British industry and commerce may ever prove the safest and the most advantageous investment of British capital.

Does it seem an easy thing to you to accumulate capital? Look around. See the vast numbers of persons who find it hard enough to get their daily bread, and to make the two ends meet. See the vast numbers earning a good income, yet spending it as fast as it comes, and never thinking of saving a farthing, far less of accumulating any capital. Think of the numbers who strive hard to save, but who, after succeeding for a time, are compelled to give up the attempt from sickness, misfortune, or losses. Think of the vicissitudes of trade, changes of fashion, and new inventions which from time to time disconcert the best conceived plan. What violent efforts, and what sudden collapses, what heaving and subsiding, what flow and ebb of fortune, do we witness! How many try, how few succeed! It is easy comparatively to accumulate after a good foundation has been laid; but how hard it is to lay that foundation. What judgment, what decision of will, what disposition to economise, there must exist to have the slightest chance of success. Doubtless the present division of property is not all that could be wished. The laws of primogeniture and entail favour the accumulation of wealth, at least in land, in comparatively few hands. Those rich enough to pay income tax on any amount of profits of trade and industry are only about 16 for every 1000 of the population of Great Britain, and of these much less than one in 1,000 (0·65) pay on incomes amounting to

£1,000, and upward, per annum. Yet the number of capitalists might be immensely greater were there more thrift, more common prudence, and more practical wisdom among the people. I do not speak of the working classes only, but of the middle and higher classes quite as much, or more. Would that they had the wisdom to lay by something for a rainy day when they have a chance of doing so! Would that they used and not abused the means which Providence places within their reach!

Realize, I pray you, what capital really is, and what a useful commodity it is to every nation. Generally speaking, capital is that portion of an individual's or of a nation's wealth which is applied to reproduction. All property becomes capital so soon as it, or the value received from it, is set apart for productive employment. By dint of industry, a shilling to-day, a pound to-morrow, you gather £100. You resolve to have a home of your own, and to employ £25 in furnishing it, and with the £75 remaining you determine to set up a shop. You have got, indeed, £100 of your own, but only £75 of capital. Just as wealth, in its economic meaning, consists of all those things, and those things only, which are transferable, limited in supply, and directly or indirectly productive of value, so capital, which is part of that wealth, must bear the same characteristic. There are many things most valuable in themselves, which are not, in their strict economic sense, capital. Capital does not include the instruments furnished by nature, without our aid. The water of the sea, the air we breathe, are not capital, unless, indeed, by labour we enclose a portion of the sea, or introduce the air into a building. Capital consists of those things which are created, and which were previously accumulated by man. To be capital, moreover, the possession must be a material object, and capable of transfer. The skill of an artist, the genius of a composer, the wisdom of a statesman, the talent of a man of letters, the health and strength of a labourer, are doubtless so many valuable endowments to their respective possessors, but they are not of a material character, and cannot be transferred. If English statesmen could transfer a little of their wisdom to the French; if British labourers could endow their *confrères* in France with a little of their strength and steadiness of purpose; if French artizans could pass over to British artizans part of their fertility of invention, and their quickness of perception, what a market there would be for them all! But these personal endowments cannot be sold or bought, and, therefore, they do not come within the meaning of the word capital.

I do not know what we should do without capital. The riches of nature are profusely scattered, some on the surface and some on the very bowels of the earth; and human labour is required to make them subservient to the many uses for which they are adapted. Few things are the spontaneous, unaided gifts of nature, requiring no exertion for their production. Nature offers its powers and its products. Industry and labour discover their latent utility, and surmount the difficulties of obtaining such products, and of giving them their requisite modification.

> "I know a bank whereon the wild thyme blows,
> Where ox-lips and the nodding violet grows ;
> Quite over-canopied with luscious woodbine,
> With sweet musk-roses, and white eglantine." *

Yet who is ignorant of the wonders of gardening? What triumphs of skill do we see in a streak, a tint, a shade secured by the morning care, the evening caution, and the vigilance of days bestowed by the diligent horticulturist.

Even labour, however, cannot always act singly. It needs the aid of tools, implements, and machines. There are in the United Kingdom immense tracts of cultivable land. Will it do simply to employ any number of men or women to till, to plough, to sow, to reap? No. The farmer must erect the

* Shakspeare.

steadings. He must clear and drain. He must eradicate noxious weeds, must make the road, the bank, the fence, the bridge. He must purchase guano or some other fertilizer. He must have a sufficient number of live stock. He must have the grubber, the roller, the harrow, the rake, the reaping machine, the thrashing machine ; ay, even the steam plough, and the steam engine, if he can afford it. How can these be obtained, unless there be something left of previous accumulation whereby to get them? Now that something is—Capital. The labourers in the act of producing must be fed and clothed. From whom can they expect their sustenance but from the capitalist? The very first use of capital, therefore, is to provide such commodities as are employed in producing wealth and in supplying the fund necessary for supporting labour.

Capital is used in all manner of ways for purposes of reproduction. We often see our manufacturers intentionally destroying it, in order to obtain the effects which are the direct consequences of its destruction ; as, for example, they consume coal in the furnace that they may produce iron. They are content to see capital used up little by little as in machinery, or consent to vary its very kind by manufacturing, or shaping it in new forms, as in the case of cotton, wool, or other raw material. Subject certain quantities of cotton and wool to certain processes ; destroy, in fact, their identity, and you obtain in their stead shirts, drawers, gloves, shawls, stockings, hose. Subject wool and woollen yarn to other processes, and you have Brussels carpets, tapestry, velvets, felt, blankets, beavers, flannel, coverlets, etc. Capital is given away in wages as reward for labour. It is employed in providing, extracting, or producing materials, as in agriculture, mining, fisheries, manufactures. It is invested in roads, railways, shipping. But in whatever way it is employed, capital is the spring, the mover of labour, and scarcely any work can be accomplished without t. The greater, indeed, the amount of capital accumulated, the larger the amount of work executed. What egregious folly it is to call capital the natural foe of labour, and the capitalist the jealous rival of labour. Instead of being an incubus on the energies of the labourer, or the weight that crushes him down, capital is the very prop and stay of labour, it is the indispensable means of all employment, and of all reward of labour.

But there is a difference in the method of employing capital. On a closer examination of what is required for production, in the very instances already given, you will find that part of the capital is employed in works of a permanent character, and part for temporary and fluctuating purposes. If you wish to establish a cotton mill, you must needs build the factory and purchase the machinery; if you will construct iron works, you must have the furnaces; if you will give yourself to agriculture, you must improve the land. Now capital so employed cannot be withdrawn at pleasure. It is for all practical purposes sunk; and all you may derive from it is a yearly rent or interest. This is technically called fixed capital. But to work the factory, to produce iron, to cultivate grain or fruit, you must get the raw material, pay wages, buy the seed, and provide for the thousand requirements of the business. And this is circulating or floating capital. The fixed capital of the hunter consists of his gun and dog; the floating, of powder and shot. The boat and net are the fixed capital of the fisherman; any food in the boat is the floating. The warehouse is the fixed capital of the trader, and so are his weights or machines; his stock in trade and effects are his floating capital. There is this further difference between fixed and circulating capital, that whilst the fixed always remains, the circulating is always spent. You buy land for a railway, that land remains. You pay money in wages, it goes. Do not imagine, however, that what is termed fixed capital is absolutely fixed or indestructible, or that what is termed floating is really lost. In truth, the fixed capital, unless renewed, is in time completely lost. The floating, though temporarily departing, always returns. That the whole floating capital employed, together with a certain amount of profits, shall return, is the whole aim of the capitalist. Alas if it does not return! And remember, too, that as all fixed capital must come originally from the operation of circulating capital, and must be fed by it, —no factory, no machine being obtainable except by first providing, and afterwards sustaining, labour,—so no fixed capital can, by any possible means, give a revenue except by the use of circulating capital; for what is the use of building the factory, or purchasing a piece of land, unless you are able and prepared to manufacture cotton or woollen, or to cultivate the ground? At home and abroad, wherever this wonderful element, capital, is distributed, it is employed as floating and as fixed in certain proportions, not always precisely the same, but still pretty well balanced. In truth, it is quite a misadventure when either form takes an undue share of public attention. Suppose, for instance the construction of public works should require the conversion of any considerable part of floating into fixed capital, and what follows? There will be much less left for the general wants of trade and ordinary purposes of manufacture, and serious inconvenience may ensue from it.

I wish I could give you some idea of the extraordinary sums of capital required to carry on the industries of this country. There are in the United Kingdom some 47,000,000 acres of land under cultivation, on which farmers sometimes invest £10 or £15 per acre. Allow £5 10s. per acre on the average, and you have £258,000,000 required for agriculture. We have a large number of industries whose very existence depends on the constant flow of capital. Some £80,000,000 sterling are required for the cotton manufacture; some £40,000,000 for the woollen; some £30,000,000 for the iron industry; some £70,000,000 for our mercantile marine. Just imagine the amount required to carry on the foreign trade of the country --those distant trades, especially, with Australia, India, China, and Japan, which do not allow of quick returns. As many as £600,000,000 of capital are invested in our railways, and I cannot tell you how much has been invested by British capitalists in public undertakings for water, gas, and docks, in banking and insurance, and in a hundred other objects at home and abroad. Yes, abroad also; for immense sums of capital are constantly going out from Britain to every part of the world, to fructify the soil of native industry, to fill waste places, and to construct great public works. And what a drain is caused by foreign loans, that new, and in many respects novel, species of gambling of the present day. Scarcely a year passes but we have princes and potentates, wealthy states and puny republics, knocking at the door of the British Stock Exchange for a new loan. At this moment, a large portion of the debt of most states in the world, probably £300,000,000, and more, is due to British capitalists. This is the way in which capital is employed. It will not do to keep capital idle, for idleness is sure to bring about its own punishment. Take it into your head that you will not work, and of course you get no wages. That is your well-deserved punishment. Let capital be kept idle, and it will bring no interest. That is its punishment. It would be interesting to know in what proportion capital is employed respectively in British industry, commerce, and shipping, and foreign enterprises and loans. I will not venture on bold estimates, but what is it that determines what specific investment shall be preferred? Nothing else than what offers the best advantage. It is the same with large as with small transactions. A fourth or a half per annum per cent. will turn the scale, whether I will buy American or British funded securities. One or two per cent. will determine whether agriculture or manufactures shall be preferred. It is wonderful what a little difference often turns the scale. But, mind you, it makes all the difference to those who are to participate in the benefit arising from the employment of capital, how capital is eventually invested.

There is a great difference, for instance, in the various proportions in which capital is distributed among the several agents of production even as between different industries. It has been calculated in France, that for every hundred francs produced, fifteen go in labour, fifty-five in materials, and the remainder in the maintenance of fixed capital, fuel, administration, and profits. According to the census of the United States for 1870, out of $100 produced, eighteen go in labour, fifty-six in raw materials, and the rest in interest and administration. What are the proportions in England it is difficult to say, but all industries are not alike. In industries where the material is of no great value, the proportion falling on labour for wages may even exceed the proportion required for the material. But there are industries of just the reverse character, where the value of the material far exceeds every other element in the cost of production. In the production of flour, which is only a process in the further utilization of wheat, in calico-printing, bleaching, and dyeing, in the reduction of gold and silver, in the refining of sugar, the proportion of the produce falling on wages is comparatively small, in some cases four, six, and eight per cent., and no more. In the production of hardwares, glass wares, furniture, cotton goods, bricks, and ship-building, the proportion of the product falling on labour ranges from twenty to thirty per cent. I have often been struck at the incongruity exhibited by a man constantly touching gold and silver, silk or woollen, of the finest description, yet he himself poor and half-starving. Walk to Spitalfields, and see the poor silk weaver: he is manufacturing some magnificent velvet, or some splendid moire antique; he must be a trusty man, for he is trusted with the material in his own home; he must have considerable knowledge of his work, and he must be at great expense in the maintenance of the loom, and even in house rent, for he must have as much space and light as he can. Ask what are his wages, and he will tell you that he has the poorest wages, often not better than a common labourer can earn. Go to a cotton factory, and you see men and women apparently simply watching a machine, or performing some mechanical act, now taking a lump of cotton from one place to another, and again replacing a single thread on the spindle. Ask what is their earning, and you will find that they get handsome wages. Why this difference? In the one case the raw material is very dear, and takes away considerable part of the produce; in the other it is very cheap, and leaves a good share to be divided among the workers. The dearer the raw material, whether ordinarily or exceptionally, the worse for the labourer and the manufacturer, for often in the difficulty of obtaining the full price the only alternative left is to work at reduced wages and profits. Happily, in England, the great bulk of our manufactures are the products of raw materials of comparatively little value. Whilst France is the home of the silk manufacture, England is the seat of the cotton and iron industries. It will not do, however, to say we should pick and choose the industries which give the best return to labour. Whatever is most beneficial to capital must also be equally beneficial to labour, and you may be sure of this, that the watchful eye of the capitalist will ever be on the outlook to make a good selection for his investments.

It is difficult to say what we should most dread, either an unlimited growth of capital, or any sudden stoppage of accumulation; for an unlimited growth would inevitably be followed by a diminution of profit, and a consequent discouragement of industry; and a diminution of capital would have results still more disastrous. As yet, we are thankful to say, there is no danger either of the one or of the other. Capital is growing in England at an enormous ratio. But the demand for capital both at home and abroad is greater than ever. Nor is it a bad thing, after all, that some of our surplus should find its way abroad. John Stuart Mill attributed to the perpetual overflow of capital to colonies or to foreign countries, to seek higher profits than can be obtained at home, the principal cause by which the decline of profits in England has been arrested. This, he said, has a twofold operation. "In the first place, it does what a fire, or an inundation, or a commercial crisis, would have done;—it carries off a part of the increase of capital from which the reduction of profits proceeds. Secondly, the capital so carried off is not lost, but is chiefly employed either in founding colonies, which become large exporters of cheap agricultural produce, or in extending, and perhaps improving, the agriculture of older communities. It is to the emigration of English capital, that we have chiefly to look for keeping up a supply of cheap food and cheap materials of clothing, proportioned to the increase of our population: thus enabling an increasing capital to find employment in the country, without reduction of profits, in producing manufactured articles with which to pay for this supply of raw produce. Thus, the exportation of capital is an agent of great efficacy in extending the field of employment for that which remains; and it may be said truly, that up to a certain point, the more capital we send away the more we shall possess and be able to retain at home." Fear not, indeed, the exportation of capital, so long as it goes to fertilize the land, to create new means of transport, to animate industry, and to strengthen and invigorate labour in America, India, Australia, or any part of the world. But fear such exportation when it goes to act as the sinews of war, when it is to be employed for destruction, and not for production. Better far to sink capital into the deep, than to lend it to any power in Europe—ay, to the British Government itself—for the support of a warlike policy in any quarter, and for any purpose whatever.

It is good, after all, to be able to say that, however selfish and materialistic it may seem at first sight, political economy has this redeeming characteristic, that it does not teach us to hide our light under a bushel, to keep what we have to ourselves and for ourselves. If you have gathered capital, let it out; do not keep it in your pocket, nor hide it in an old stocking. If you have any talent, let it shine. Use it liberally for yourselves and for others. I remember reading a happy illustration of the principle in question as applied to literary pursuits in "Excelsior," a charming publication, edited by the late Dr. Hamilton. "An earnest mind," he said, "is not a bucket, but a fountain; and as good thoughts flow out, better thoughts flow in. Good thoughts are gregarious. The bright image or sparkling aphorism, the gold or silver of capital,—fear not to give it wing, for, lured by its decoy, thoughts of sublimer range and sunnier pinion will be sure to descend and gather round it. As you scatter, you'll increase. And it is in this way that, whilst many a thought that might have enriched the world has been buried in a sullen and monastic spirit, like a crock of gold in a coffin, the good idea of a frank and forth-spoken man gets currency, and after being improved to the advantage of thousands, has returned to its originator with usury. It has been lent, and so it has not been lost; it has been communicated, and so it has been preserved; it has circulated, and so it has increased."

We should all remember that, in one sense or another, we are all capitalists. In an economic sense, labour is an element distinct from capital. But in a better sense—for it is the sense of common experience—we stand much more on a level. We are all labourers, and all capitalists. Taking the working classes at two-thirds of the entire population, and assuming an average weekly aggregate earning of thirty shillings for each family of 4·50 persons, the entire income of the working classes will amount to £400,000,000 per annum, probably quite as much as the income of all the middle and higher classes together. You, the working classes, destitute of all capital, a class distinct from the capitalists? What folly! Multiply that earning of yours at ten years' purchase, and your property in your labour income from all sources is worth £4,000,000,000. Away with all jealousy between Labour and Capital! We are all interested in each other's welfare: on the success of the capitalist your income depends; and on your welfare and happiness, the capitalist's chief strength must ever rest.

Moralists have often been led to decry the all-absorbing eagerness of the present age in the pursuit of wealth, and fears have been expressed lest the love of money should engross far too much the heart and mind of the nation,—lest, instead of seeking wealth as an instrument for the purchase of ease and enjoyment, both the ease and the enjoyment of a whole life should be rendered up a sacrifice to its shrine,—lest, instead of its being desired as a minister of gratification to the appetites of nature, it should bring nature itself into bondage, robbing her of all her simple delights, pouring wormwood into the current of her feelings, making that man sad who ought to be cheerful. Well might Matthew Henry say, "There is a burden of care in getting riches; fear in keeping them; temptation in using them; guilt in abusing them; sorrow in losing them; and a burden of account at last to be given up concerning them."

But let us not ignore or forget the many benefits derived from wealth; and whilst we condemn an excessive devotion to its pursuit, let us be ready to acknowledge that the acquisition of wealth is good in itself as the reward of well-directed labour, of industry, frugality, and economy. And look at the results! What power of attraction, what magic influence, does capital possess! What wonders does it achieve! Behold the embodiments of capital in our halls and palaces, docks and warehouses, factories and workshops, railways and canals, parks and pleasure grounds. What a mighty power is capital, even in politics! Three millions of British sovereigns have silenced the grumbling of the Americans for the concession of belligerent rights to the Confederate States, and the raids of the *Alabama* and other privateers on American shipping. Four millions of hard sovereigns have procured to England an interest in the Suez Canal. What is it that renders Britain so influential in the council of the nations? What is it that placed this nation, once so obscure, in the foremost place in civilization and science? Whence, but by the expenditure of much treasure, has Britain been rendered the healthy and courted resort of princes and nobles from all countries? Look around, and see what wealth is capable of performing,—what monuments it has raised,—what agencies it has called into activity,—what encouragement it has afforded to science, art, and discoveries. What but wealth has procured for Britain those store-houses of knowledge which enrich our museums and galleries? And what but the existence of a class in the full enjoyment of ease and wealth has given to the nation the immense benefit of a large number of men who, with refined taste and enlarged views, can give themselves to those higher objects which foster civilization and science? It is the glory of England that she possesses so many men of position and wealth, who, eschewing the temptation of ease and luxury, are thankful if they are selected to preside over our hospitals, to take their share in the maintenance of order and justice, to devote themselves to legislation, to take an active part in the laborious task of our School Boards.

Many are the examples of liberality, moreover, which redeem wealth from the charge of sordid avarice or cold unconcern for human suffering. The names of George Moore and George Peabody, of Samuel Morley and the Baroness Coutts, are household words in the national catalogue of benefactors:—

> "Those are great souls, who touch'd with warmth divine,
> Give gold a price, and teach its beams to shine ;
> All hoarded pleasures they repute a load,
> Nor think their wealth their own, till well bestow'd."

And let any cry of distress be heard, do we not see at once a flow of liberality to mitigate its pressure? Yes! let wealth continue to diffuse blessings such as these, and what a crop of beneficence will be gathered! How much misery will be alleviated! What amount of ignorance will be removed! What high purposes will be served! In the work of production and distribution of wealth, most of us are immediately interested. Let us be thankful for the measure of prosperity this work of ours procures for us. Let us remember that, whether rich or poor in gold and silver, it is always in our power to possess the godlike happiness of doing good, to be benefactors to others, and to have a perpetual spring of peace and joy in ourselves.

IV.

THE REWARD OF LABOUR.

ARE the working classes at this moment receiving such wages as they are entitled to have ? Do they participate fully and justly in the produce of their labour ? Do they get a just reward for the work they perform? These are the questions before us this evening ; and certainly I know of no other social theme which has called forth more continuous, more keen, and more interesting controversy. We all know that labour is indispensable for production,—that it must be performed with energy, health, and intelligence,—that it is economised by machinery, and rendered more productive by the division of labour,—and that, as a whole, labour is exercised in England under circumstances, physical, economical, and political, far superior to those of many other countries. Now let us bring labour face to face with capital, that element so much dreaded for its power and influence, yet without which labour cannot proceed. On the one hand, we have the labourer hard at work in the business of life ; on the other, the capitalist, bringing to the help of labour the fruit of his saving, yet trying to economise it, and to render it as useful as possible. Labourers both they are, the labourer and the capitalist, because all capital is the fruit of labour—saved, not wasted, and employed in reproduction. Whilst, however, there lie before us the two parties in the great conflict, ever at issue, ever jealous of one another, and now and again coming to an open struggle, let us keep in mind that the two great factors in the determination of the reward of labour, are not capital and labour, but the producers on the one hand, as including both labour and capital, and the consumers on the other. On what condition can the interests of all parties be satisfactorily established, and any seeming divergence reconciled?

I do not know how far you are prepared to give heed to what economists have to say on a question which so touches your interest to the quick. I have heard the science charged with being cold and unsympathetic, yet I believe that its dictates ought to be listened to with attention, for Adam Smith and John Stuart Mill, Jean Baptiste Say and Michel Chevalier, did not give their oracles as from the gods, but as the result of induction from ascertained facts. And whence the immense accumulation of wealth within the last quarter of a century, in which the labouring classes have so much participated, but from the recognition of the principles of economic science and the practical application of their dictates to national legislation?

The machinery of production and distribution is much more complicated than we are apt to imagine, for it extends back to the manifold operations connected with the production and acquisition of the raw materials, tools, and factories, and reaches far and away, through manifold ramifications, till the produce finds its way into the hands of the consumer. In a primitive state of society, a labourer may easily cut a tree and build a hut for himself, or work on the virgin soil and draw from it a scanty subsistence; but it is not so in the present advanced civilization. The raw materials come from the most distant regions. The tools, machines, and instruments are the products of exquisite skill. The motive power is no longer the running steam or the rushing wind. How extensive, how systematic, how economically adapted everything must be ere a labourer can enter into his labour! What scheming, what organization, what foresight are required in the master in the conduct of all his operations! What a number of agents! How many are the instrumentalities required to bring the produce within the reach of the consumer, in towns and hamlets, at home and abroad! Travel among the Exquimaux or the Hottentots, penetrate Asia or America, visit the Fair of Nijni Novgorod, and the bazaars at Constantinople, and everywhere you find British goods. How came they there? What toil, what expenditure to bring them there! How much of the produce of such goods falls into the hands of the producer in England, and how much is divided and subdivided among the merchants and traders, carriers and shipmasters, agents and brokers, engaged in their transmission, who can say?

Nor is it easy to ascertain how the net amount which eventually falls into the hands of the producer should be distributed between the master and the workmen, the capitalist and the labourer. Deeply interested alike in the results of production, interdependent on one another for its success, we might fancy they might easily agree to act jointly in a kind of partnership. But can the labourer wait till the article is completed and sold, to divide the proceeds with the capitalist? Can he work on the chance that the article may be sold or prove profitable? Better for him, in most cases, to receive something prompt and certain, than a larger sum at a distant time, and contingent on the success of the enterprise. Nor would such an agreement answer the interest of the master, for he must look to the best time for selling his merchandize, and he cannot expose himself to the pressure of the labourers, or to the danger of disagreement. Better for them both to substitute for such an uncertain issue, which might in the end prove satisfactory to neither party, the contract of wages, or the purchase and sale of certain labour for a certain renumeration, the workmen consenting to have their share of the profits, whatever they be, or their chance of profit or loss, commuted into a fixed payment. Only let it be understood that in entering into such a contract the parties agree on the mutual recognition of property in capital and labour, and on the absolute freedom on the part of both, the one to demand, and the other to give, whatever their respective interests may dictate.

The business of production is one requiring extreme nicety of calculation. To accept a contract for the building of a house, to undertake the working of a mill, or to rent a farm, are alike operations the success of which depends on the careful estimate of receipts and expenditure. We often speak of the master as the capitalist, but the capital he requires is a commodity having a market value, and the cost of which he must take into account. You wish to establish a cotton mill: the mill itself may cost you some £30,000 in land, buildings, steam-engines, gas-works, warehouses, and all the fixed requisites, besides a per centage per annum for repair and dilapidation. Beyond this, as much capital will be required for the machinery; and to that, too, a still larger per centage per annum must be added for wear and tear, and renewal when worked out. Then you need capital to purchase cotton and stock for carrying on the trade. You have the insurance to pay, and the expense of taxes, engines, horses, the weekly contengencies of oil, tallow, etc.; and the most important item, the interest of all this capital, which varies from time to time from $2\frac{1}{2}$ to 10 per cent. per annum. Add now, the wages of labour, and the remuneration due to the master for the labour and talent required in the administration,—talent often of a very high order,—and you can form a fair estimate of the cost of the article produced. But can the manufacturer count upon recovering the whole of his cost from the consumer? Ultimately, indeed, the value of any article is regulated by the cost of production, whatever that be; but is there no probability that the competition between the producers within the same or in different countries, or the inability of the consumers, may compel the producer to sell at prices lower than he had calculated. And if so, the cost of capital and other commodities being the same, must not the master, if he is to continue to produce, lower the wages of labour and be content to do himself with less remuneration?

It is objected, that before thinking of lowering the wages, the master should see whether some economy might not be effected in the expense of distribution, which often absorbs so large a portion of the produce of an article. It is possible that some economy may be effected in this direction, but in this matter the producer is often helpless, the business of production being quite distinct from that of distribution. Do not imagine that it would be economy if the producer should attempt to take into his own hands the business of distribution, for would he not require double the number of agents, a corresponding increase in the amount of capital, and double the amount of profits? But allowing the necessity of lowering both profits and wages, it is asserted that it must still remain at the option of the workman whether he will sell his labour at the lower rates. No one can certainly question the right of the workman to act on his own judgment in the matter. All I venture to assert is that the master may be compelled by the circumstances of trade to offer to his workmen less wages for the future than he was wont to give for the past. If they will not accept such lower wages, the master cannot help it, but the chances are that if they insist on refusing the offer production may be thereby suspended, for surely the master may be credited for using the best means in his power to carry on his business, not only without interruption, but in peace and harmony with his men, if he can possibly do so.

The motive power which prompts a master in accepting a contract for the building of a house, in undertaking the working of a mill, or the renting of a farm, is doubtless profit. It is with a view to profit that he emplo· his own capital, and whatever additional capital may be required in his business; and it is with a view to profit that he employs his labourers. To succeed the master must seek to economise the use of every element which affects the cost of the produce; must choose the best market for it; must endeavour to maintain his productive power, and avoid any break or interruption of work. But do you think that it is the interest of the employer to starve his labourers? I venture to say, the employer is fully conscious of the fact that those whom he employs, must be able to live by their work, that they must educate their children, and they must have a share of relaxation and enjoyment, without which life becomes a burden. The master cannot forget that the best way to make his labourers work well is to pay them well, or as well as the state of business permits, to keep them happy and cheerful, strong and healthy; and he knows, too, full well, that if he will deal justly by his labourers, they will neither neglect their work nor be disaffected, they will neither complain nor be disposed to strike. Only, the master cannot always control the course of the market, and he may be compelled to lower the wages and reduce his profits, lest by keeping the cost of production too high, he should become unable to compete with the foreign producers, or to meet the ability of the consumers, and so lose his custom altogether.

Where is the guarantee, however, that the employer will act fairly in such calculations? What if his intentions be solely to force the labourers to accept lower wages with a view to the retention of higher profits? What if the statements of bad trade, or restricted demand, or increasing competition, should be purposely exaggerated for the same end? What, in short, if the wages offered are not justified by the state of the market? I fully admit the possibility of such circumstances, and I think that where there has been between masters and men a long course of dealings, the men have a moral right to expect from the master an open and frank statement of the position of the business, and of the reasons which necessitate an alteration of the terms of their contract, before he summarily announces a reduction of wages. In any case, he should remember that he has to deal with his labourers as with free men, and that they will exercise their judgment to accept or not, as they please, the wages offered. And be sure of this, that if the competition among labourers is certain to prove favourable to the employer in keeping the wages low, the freedom of the labourers, and an extensive field of labour in the colonies and America, enable the labourers to resist any attempt of his to lower wages unduly, and to prevent them falling below what is just and necessary.

There is, indeed, a minimum below which wages can never go. Much labour has been expended in ascertaining what that minimum is, or what is the intrinsic value of labour at any time; and it has been said that, as the intrinsic value of anything is regulated by the cost of production, so the intrinsic value of labour is ultimately governed by the cost of subsistence of the labourer and his family. However large the competition among labourers, the wages can never fall below the cost of bare living, for the simple reason that if the labourer cannot live in one occupation, he will leave it and choose another; and if he is not able for any other, he will emigrate. This, then, is the natural or necessary rate of wages, and it is variable according to the cost of articles of food and clothing, and must also differ at different times and in different countries. Let it be established, for instance, that the cost of living in England, including food, drink, clothing, and house-rent, has increased twenty per cent. within the last twenty years, and the natural or intrinsic value of labour must of necessity have risen in similar proportions.* And must not the intrinsic value of labour be higher in England, where the labourer eats wheaten bread

* See Appendix A.

and butcher's meat daily, than in China, where a labourer is content and able to live almost exclusively on rice?

Happily, this minimum of wages is scarcely ever touched, but there are industries where the profits of production are extremely low, and where the competition among labourers is extreme. Who has not heard of the pitiful cases of the silk weavers and throwsters, of the needlewomen and kid-glove stitchers, of the stocking and glove weavers, of the farm and dock labourers? It does seem miserable pay to offer $2\frac{1}{2}d.$ for embroidering a skirt two or three yards wide, even with the sewing machine. Who has not felt pain, sorrow, and I may say indignation, when reading those plaintive words of Hood:

> " With fingers weary and worn,
>   With eyelids heavy and red,
> A woman sat, in unwomanly rags,
>   Plying her needle and thread—
>   Stitch! stitch! stitch!
> In poverty, hunger, and dirt;
>   And still with a voice of dolorous pitch
> She sang the 'Song of the Shirt.'
>
> Work, work, work—
>   Till the brain begins to swim!
> Work, work, work—
>   Till the eyes are heavy and dim!
> Seam, and gusset, and band,
> Band, and gusset, and seam—
>   Till over the buttons I fall asleep,
> And sew them on in a dream!"

But what is the cause of such low wages? Some say, nothing else but the competition among producers to sell their products sufficiently cheap to attract custom. But pay higher wages, and immediately a rise on the price of such articles must be made, which will lessen proportionally their consumption, and check likewise production. Do not say that the consumers would pay more if they could not get such articles so cheap. Probably a great number will, but a large number will abstain from consuming them. The consumption of articles of necessity, as well as of luxury, is alike governed by the price. Add a penny to the cost of a single shirt, or to that of a pound of tea, or a halfpenny to the price of sugar or a loaf of bread, and at once the consumption is sure to diminish in exact proportion. And what will be the consequence? A reduction of production means a less demand for labour; and many who are now obtaining a scanty livelihood, may, instead of getting more, be doomed to get nothing at all. The wages of agricultural labour are low, but remember that in most cases the labour is purely manual, and that the supply of simply manual labour is always superabundant. Mr. Malthus exhibited with great force the disagreeable fact, that, whilst the population is capable of increasing at a geometrical ratio, such as 2, 4, 8, 16, 32, and so forth, the means of subsistence only increase at an arithmetical ratio such as 1, 2, 3, 4, 5, etc. Doubtless, a proper restraint in the matter of matrimony, and prudence as regards the increase of our families, might check the excess of labourers, and so tend to keep wages above their minimum, but we cannot trust on so much wisdom on the part of the people, and so our only hope must lie in the vast fields of emigration ever open for our superabundant population. As an evidence that supply and demand of labour regulate the wages compare Devon and Northumberland. In Devon the wages are, say, 12s. a week; in Northumberland, 20s. But in Devon the supply of labour is far in excess of the demand; in Northumberland, with the demand for coal-mining, and with Newcastle at hand, full of industries absorbing any quantity of labour, labour is ever scarce. What is it that lowers so much the wages in the manufacturing districts but the constant influx of agricultural labourers? As Mr. Cobden tersely put it, when two workmen run after one master, the wages will fall; and when two masters run after a workman, the wages are certain to rise.

There are industries, however,—and I am happy to say they

include almost every branch of the artisan population,—where the wages are not pressed down by excessive supply of labour, and where fair wages ought to obtain. To be remunerative the wages ought to provide the workman not only the cost of living to himself and his family in the locality where the workman must live,—in London, if his work be there, or in a provincial town, if his labour be there,—but also the cost and maintenance of his tools, the recovery of the cost of his apprenticeship, some provision for old age and infirmity, and an insurance against the perils of sudden or early death, especially in those occupations which are essentially injurious to health. And some difference should be made, too, for the agreeableness or disagreeableness of the work. But all these items are represented in the relative wages of different classes of artisans. What is included in the price of an article, in a certain rate of wages of labour, in the course of exchange between one country and another, or in the rate of interest on capital, it is often extremely difficult to analyse. The Bank rate is, say, $3\frac{1}{2}$ per cent. In what proportions are included in that rate the value of capital proper, the commission and expense of the transaction, and the insurance of the risk? And so as regard wages. How much, for instance, of the ninepence per hour goes to meet the relation of supply and demand of masons or carpenters, the cost of their tools, and any of the other considerations named? Such analyses are not easily made, yet depend upon it the wages or the price represents the aggregate of all the items which enter into their value at the time.

It should be remembered that whilst the labourer calculates what he receives in relation to the compensation he expects for his work and toil, the employer calculates what he gives in relation to the amount of work performed for him in return; for the same amount of wages may produce twice as much labour where the labourer is sturdier in strength, and really in earnest in his work, than where the labourer is weak and indolent. And is there not a difference in the power of labour between the stalwart Northumbrian and the weakly Devonian? A greater amount of labour will be performed in a summer than in a winter's day, in countries where the people are less given to enjoyments than in those where pleasure seems the first and most attractive pursuit. Let us suppose that in France, Austria, or any other country, a manufacturer should require twice the number of hands, twice as large a building to contain the hands, twice as many clerks and bookkeepers and overlookers to look after them, and twice as many tools as he would to do the same quantity of work in England, must he not pay such labourers less there than he would here? The rate of wages may be lower in France than in England, and yet the amount of wages paid for a given quantity of work may be more in France than in England. " Profits," said Mr. Ricardo, " depend on wages,—not on nominal but real wages ; not on the number of pounds that may be annually paid to the labourers, but on the number of days' work necessary to obtain those pounds."

By whichever standard the rate of wages may be estimated, the question really at issue between masters and men is whether or not what is now paid in the shape of wages is just, or below what is really due to the share taken by labour in production. There is no concealing the fact that in the mind of many of our workmen there is a lurking idea that the immense fortunes amassed by our producers and traders are more or less the result of an unequal division of the profits of production, and that they could pay considerably more wages, but they will not. That indeed, they say, is the real secret of low wages. Only, they try to cover it under the pretext of the doctrine of the wages or labour fund. But what is this theory? According to the economists, the doctrine is simply this : that wages, by an irresistible law, depend on the demand and supply of labour, and can in no circumstances be either more or less than what will distribute the existing wage fund among the existing number of competitors for the same,—the demand for labour consisting of the whole circulating capital of the country, including what is paid in wages for unproductive labour; the supply, the whole labouring population. If the supply is in excess of what the capital can at present employ, wages must fall. If the labourers are all employed, and there is a surplus of capital still unused, wages will rise. This is the wage-fund theory upon which Mr. Thornton broke lance with John Stuart Mill. If the question be asked, Is there such a thing as a wage fund, in the sense here implied? exists there any fixed amount which is neither more nor less than what is destined to be expended in wages? Mr. Thornton boldly declares that the supposed barrier to the expansion of wages as indicated by this theory is a shadow, and not a reality, for besides the original capital which the employer invests in the business, there are the growing profits which may also be used in wages. Mr. Mill, in his review of Mr. Thornton's work on "Labour and its Claims," in the *Fortnightly Review*, so far admitted that there is no law of nature making it impossible for wages to rise to the point of absorbing not only the funds which the employer had intended to devote to the carrying on his business, but the whole of what he allows for his private expenses beyond the necessaries of life. But, said Mr. Mill, there is a limit nevertheless, and that limit to the rise of wages is the practical consideration how much would ruin the employer, or drive him to abandon his business. In short, just as wages may be too low, so as to impair the working power of the labourer, so they may be too high, so as to leave no profit; and just as excessively low wages will drive the labourer to emigrate, so unduly high wages will drive capital out of the business.

How far the assumption is correct that employers are amassing large profits, I am not prepared to say. The understanding is, that the return of seven per cent. on the capital invested is a ple, and it cannot be considered excessive when we consider the dangers and vicissitudes of commerce. See what losses are incurred by bankruptcy. During the last six years, from 1870 to 1875, the total amount of liabilities of estates liquidated by bankruptcy, by arrangement, or composition with creditors, was £110,759,000, and the total amount of assets £32,607,000, showing an actual loss to creditors of £78,152,000, or in the proportion of £13,000,000 per annum; and this, remember, irrespective of the cost of bankruptcy, which in many cases absorbs nearly the whole of the assets. Suppose, however, good fortune should favour any branch of production, and unusual profits be realised, will there not be a sudden rush of capital for investment in the same? For a time, the greedy employer may pocket large profits, but as soon as fresh capital is invested, competition causes a larger share of the same to fall on the labourer, and wages rise, till the rates of profits and the rates of wages are brought to their normal level. The relation of profits to wages is often wrongly apprehended. It is an error to suppose that large profits are the results of low wages, and low profits the results of high wages. Although an increase of capital has the tendency to lower the profits, and to increase wages, the same increase of capital also tends to render labour more profitable, and to increase the amount of production, which in turn maintains a high rate of profits. See the operation of machinery on wages. The investment of capital in machinery enables the workman to produce tenfold more than he was able to produce by the hand; and in proportion as he increases his productive power, so his earnings increase. A workman at Bristol said that the extra production of machinery ought to be divided by masters and workmen. And so they are, in certain proportions. Before 1842, said Mr. Ashworth, the operative spinner's wages for the production of 20 lb. of yarn 70's, on a pair of mules of 400 spindles each, was 4s. 7d. (or 2¾d. per lb.), and at this rate his net earnings amounted to about 20s. per week. In 1859, with the improvements effected in the spinning mule, by which each machine carries 800 spindles, the same workman, with a little extra assistance by piecers (boys), could earn 30s. 10d. per week net, although the amount he received in wages for 20 lb. of yarn was reduced from 4s. 7d. to 3s. 11¼d. or 2˙36d., per pound. Compare the actual earnings of spinners and others employed in the cotton industry during the last forty years: they show an increase of 30 or 50 per cent., besides a considerable reduction in the number of hours of labour.*

The reason why the employer amasses a larger amount of wealth in proportion than the labourer, will be found, not in any usurpation of the share of profits which may belong to workmen, for that, after all, is a matter of simple contract, but in the fact that whilst the labourer receives only the proper remuneration of his labour, the employer not only gets higher remuneration for his skill, because of a higher order, but also the profit of his capital, or an annual sum of profit on the aggregate accumulation of all his savings for years past;—to say nothing of the immense advantage of production on a large scale which the possession of large capital enables the master to realize, and of his chances of large profits from sudden changes in the value of produce, to be placed, however, against the chance of equally sudden losses, the result either of unusual skill and good fortune, or of sad miscalculations and blunders.

The wages of labour, the profits of merchants and bankers, the earnings of men of letters, of barristers and doctors, the salaries of civil servants, and even the incomes of bishops and clergymen, are not, I apprehend, so uniformly balanced as we might wish. Doubtless, the progress of freedom, the extended knowledge of the use of capital, the progress of division of labour, the facilities of communication, and the advanced con-

* See Appendix B.

dition of certain industries, may tend to the greater equalization of wages. But such equalization can never supersede the essential difference of earnings of any number of persons, the natural consequence of greater or less amount of skill, greater or less amount of energy, health, or special capacities, and of relative advantage of position for the exercise of certain industries. To suppose the possibility of any uniformity of wages, irrespective of such differences of skill, knowledge, industry, and character, is to imagine that equal enjoyment may be had as the return for unequal efforts, abilities, and sacrifices. Upon the relative merits of the payment of wages, by the day or hour, or by so-called piece-work, little need be said. The contract of labour is doubtless not so many hours, but so much labour for so much money; and it should be a matter of simple convenience to both parties which of the two systems should be preferable. Honestly performed, and as honestly inspected, piece-work appears to me to contain the elements of perfect fairness, though payment by the day may stimulate greater attention to solidity and finish of workmanship.

I will not venture to assert that present wages are satisfactory. Taking the wages of builders in the metropolis at 9d. per hour, they may appear sufficiently liberal. But are all builders earning as much? How many get no more than 7½d. per hour? How little are the building labourers earning! Nor do such wages continue uninterrupted during the year: for at least two months of the year many of them remain in forced idleness. True, the rates of wages are higher now than they were, but the cost of living has increased also, whilst the standard of living is altogether altered. Must they not pay more now for the education of their children? Can they do without their newspapers? Must they not travel from their homes to their works? And ought they not to have their due relaxation on Bank holidays, at Christmas, and Whitsuntide? Many items of expenditure, once deemed extravagant, are now become almost as imperative as the necessaries of life. And if the imperial taxes are higher, are not the local rates greatly increased? There are features at work which leave much to be desired in the economics of the labouring classes. The sudden emancipation of youth from all family control, and the consequent waste of recourses which a family purse would avoid, are a decided evil. The large proportion of married women employed in the textile industries, is a sad element in the social system. Let the man be the bread-winner, and the woman attend to household duties. That is Nature's rule; but instead of this, all home comforts are sacrificed for recruiting the scanty wages of the men, certain to be destroyed by mismanagement. Happy indeed would it be for the manufacturing districts of England were every married woman having a family prohibited working in any factory, for it is contrary to the course of all nature that mothers should have to deposit their nurslings with some friend or neighbour, or perhaps in some institution established for that purpose, whilst they go out to work for the family living.*

Better wages, and better use of wages, we must still desire. Think not that higher wages will restrain industry, for the economic condition of the masses all over the world is immensely improved, and their means of purchase are decidedly enlarged. Low wages are the concomitant of declining, not of prosperous industries. It has been said that high wages engender idleness and dissipation. I do not agree with such a proposition. Idleness and dissipation are more frequently the consequence of misery and want of strength than of comfort, health, and vigour. A sudden increase of means may, for a time, lead to extravagance, but let it consolidate itself into a regular income, and it is sure to create love of property, a desire of acquisition, and a sense of self-esteem,—the best safeguards against waste and dissipation. Charge not the recent rise of wages for the un-

* See Report of Robert Baker, Esq., Factory Inspector, 31st October, 1873, p. 120.

happy condition of large numbers of the labouring classes. Charge the same, the rather, on the want of education, on the employment of women and children in factories, and on the many evils incident to our present, in many respects, artificial organization of society.

For all the progress achieved during the last half century in the economic condition of the people, let us be thankful. What a change in the mode of living from the time of Queen Elizabeth, when, while the gentlemen provided themselves with sufficiency of wheat for their own table, their households and poor neighbours were content with rice or barley, or in time of dearth with bread made either of beans, peas, or oats. And we are cleverer, too, as to the true sources of better wages. Bitter experience has more than proved that war cannot improve the condition of the labouring classes, for whatever hinders or interrupts the production of wealth, whatever discourages the investment of capital, must of necessity reduce employment and lower wages. True, a sudden demand of men for the army and navy may cause a temporary diminution of competition among labourers; but while production is well-nigh suspended, and the unproductive expenditure excessive, the resources of the people are sure to suffer. The attempt to regulate wages by law has been tried and failed, as might have been well expected. An artificial barrier of prohibitions and import duties has been tried as a means to foster the productive power of the nation, but what is the use of producing, when the people cannot consume? The fictitious and dangerous experiment of supplementing wages by poor relief has also been tried, and abandoned as Communistic in principle, and economically most mischievous. A better era, a sounder policy, has been at last inaugurated, and wealth has increased at a rapid pace. Have the labouring classes profited by the happy change to the full extent in their power? Workmen, it is for you to answer. Are you desirous to improve your condition, to become yourselves capitalists? It is quite within your reach, for wages are the parent of all capital. Only, learn to be thrifty. Beware of little expenses, and you will soon amass capital which will enable you from labourers to become employers ; employers, I hope, the more able to deal kindly and justly with your men because you have yourselves occasionally had reason to complain of your own employers.

V.

TRADE UNIONS.

THE tree is known by its fruit. You cannot expect roses from thorns. And from a legislation which deliberately robbed the working man of the only true patrimony he possessed—his labour—by compelling him to work at such wages as the master chose to pay, by one degree only removed from the state of slavery, where both the slave and his work are the property of the master; from a legislation which consigned to the common gaol any one who attempted to improve his wages, and doomed to the pillory any one who dared attempt to conspire, covenant, or promise, with or to any other, that he should not do certain works but at certain rates, and should not work but at certain hours and time, you could expect nothing else but secret societies acting in the most arbitrary manner, discountenancing any record of their proceedings, having their most stringent laws unwritten, and their most significant usages unrecorded, whose committees were practically irresponsible, whose threats were not expressed but understood, and whose punishments were carried out, not in broad daylight, but by invisible hands. Happily, we may say, the age of secret societies is now gone by. We have no sympathy for the Templars or the Jesuits, the Red Cross or the Carbonari, and though we laugh at the Pope putting Freemasonry in the Syllabus—for we know it *not* to be any conspiracy against Government and religion, but a fraternity for the practice of mutual charity, protection, and assistance—we rejoice to know also that secret societies need no longer exist, and should have no place in the political, social, or economical condition of the nation.

There are a few, but very few, who profess to regard capitalists, as a class, with suspicion, and who account for their existence simply as an historical accident, owing its birth, perhaps, to the fact of all nations having begun in slavery. Incapable of accounting for the fact that for every hundred persons ninety-six are working people and four capitalists, such enthusiasts are prepared, like Caspar Rauchbilder, a kind of philosophic sugar-baker, to put society into a cauldron, secure a perfect vacuum by relieving it of all prejudices and all property, and from the ashes make a filter, through which this selfish age shall pass, and emerge a new moral world. But the great mass of members of our Trade Societies are not such foolish dreamers. If they fail at all, they fail in contemplating capital as something to a certain extent antagonistic to labour,—in striving *not* for a maximum of production, but for the maximum share of a given amount of production, in endeavouring to secure for labour the largest share of a product, which is, to say the least, the joint result of capital and labour. But whatever be the object, workmen have a perfect right to combine, and seek such ends as are lawful, in the way they best prefer. The right to combine with others in order to secure a common benefit is, I believe, a sacred one, not a whit less sacred than that of individual liberty; and I rejoice that all laws against combinations have long ago been abolished. Nay, I go further; I believe that the formation of Trade Societies, within proper limits, is perfectly justifiable, and may be even to some extent beneficial, for I sympathise with the condition of many of our workmen, who seldom come into direct contact with their employers, or who have to deal with masters too much hardened in the old system of ruling with the iron rod to be able fully to recognise the higher aspirations of our workmen.

Only, let me say to such societies, and more particularly to their leaders, that great as is the power of association, it cannot be all-supreme; and undoubted as is their utility, there are rights and privileges which must be likewise guarded and protected. Individual independence, and the right of isolated action, are quite as essential as the right of association, and no one ought to be called to abdicate such rights in deference to those of the association. Whilst asserting their right to act in a corporate capacity, they must not ignore the right of those who prefer to act by themselves and for themselves. Whatever be the proportion of Trade Unionists to the total number of workers in any branch of industry, this is not a case where the majority can bind the minority, simply because by no act of theirs, as in a case of partnership, can non-unionists be said to have delegated to unionists any power to interfere with their rights and independence.

Much do I deplore any contest between labour and capital. It is ominous to find, on the one hand, a National Federation of Associated Employers established with a view "to secure, through the continuance of existing laws and the enactment of new ones, complete freedom of labour, protection to capital, and the true interests of national industry," with their excellent organ *Capital and Labour;* and, on the other, "a Federation of Trade Unions," recently organized, or about to be organized, in view " that struggles between capital and labour will probably be conducted in future on a far more gigantic scale than we have hitherto witnessed, with the *Beehive*, now the *Industrial Review*, also ably conducted as *their* organ. What can we expect from two such antagonistic forces set in battle array but quarrels and conflicts? What better justification could Trade Societies have for their existence than the very fact of such associations among the masters? The masters justify their unions by the necessity of self-defence.

But what other plea is put forth by Trade Unions but self-defence? Whether or not the regulations which bind the masters associations substantially differ from those of Trade Unions is of less importance than the fact itself, that those who may be supposed to be more intelligent, and better acquainted with economic laws, find that union is strength for them as well as for others, and that instead of resting on the working of economic laws, they endeavour by united action to offer an effective resistance to the claims of labour.

But can labour effectively contend with capital? Here effective strength does not depend on mere numbers. What though the proletaires be ninety-six and the capitalists only four in a hundred? True, labour is property, and capital is property. But what is the value of labour as property unless employed by capital? As well have a Raphael in the Sandwich Islands as have ninety-six labourers without the four capitalists. And is not this superabundance of labour a constant source of weakness? Even if you succeed in regulating the supply of labour in this country, can you attempt to do so in foreign countries? True, capital can do nothing without labour, but neither can labour do anything without capital. To both capital and labour I should say, by all means use your power and energy in maintaining your rights; but avoid any resort to strikes, or the final arbitrement of war, which is sure to destroy the very spoil you are striving to possess.

Well organized as many of the Trade Societies are, I cannot help thinking that their constitution is defective, in supposing a greater equality of capacities and skill in their members than human experience justifies us in expecting, a greater amount of intelligence and prescience in their councils or committees than they can lay title to possess, and in assuming greater authority to compel obedience to their rules than is consistent with the nature of a perfectly voluntary society. The members are supposed to be, every one, able to earn the average wages which the trade gives, or the minimum wages which the Union determines, the test of that ability being found in either five years' apprenticeship or five years' work in the trade, or the testimony of any member who may have worked with the candidate. Are such tests invariably reliable? Intelligent workmanship is, I imagine, the result of qualities and circumstances not always acquired by apprenticeship, nor are many years' work in a business a sure guarantee for ability; whilst the testimony which will satisfy the committee of a Union may not be such as will satisfy an employer. Within an apparent uniformity of qualifications there may be an essential diversity of merit. Hundreds of gentlemen are called to the bar every year by the Inns of Court under the same regulations. Can it be said that they are all equally gifted? A uniform wage obtains among privates in the army, but that continues so long only as they are idling in the barracks, a mass of inert force. Let them be in active service, and immediately individual valour will show that they are not a band of uniform automatic machines.

The executive councils or committees are called to fulfil duties of a most difficult and delicate character. Their efforts are to secure a fair and reasonable remuneration for labour, to maintain a fair rate of wages, to provide the means of legally resisting unnecessary reductions in the price of work, and to allow no encroachment on the peculiar privileges of the trade. But is it an easy work to determine what is a fair rate of wages, what is a reasonable remuneration, when a reduction may be successfully resisted, or when no such resistance should be attempted? The members of council or committees are themselves workmen. They do not pretend to be guided by the theories or maxims of political economists. Naturally in favour of high wages and short hours, are they such impartial judges as to be able duly to appreciate the real circumstances of the case before acting in any emergency? True, they are guided by the periodical reports of the state of trade and wages from every part of the kingdom;

but these very facts are only the exponent of phenomena which require a deep and extended range of observation on conditions and circumstances not within the reach of every one. Far be it from me to detract from the intelligence and practical knowledge of the councils of such trade unions. I give them full credit for an earnest desire to form sound opinions on the questions before them, and to urge the same for acceptance by fair, open, and peaceful means. Only, it is not in their power to regulate economical phenomena, and they cannot prevent their action.

The societies are supported by entrance fees, by weekly or monthly fees, and by fines. Failing to pay the proper contribution, absenting oneself from a quarterly or a special meeting, mentioning any club transactions to outsiders, omitting to make a proper report, and performing many more such acts and transactions, are visited with fines; whilst a still more hostile system of ostracism may be resorted to where perfect obedience is not secured by fines. But is it desirable to enforce obedience among a large number of men on matters which touch very nearly the mode of earning a livelihood? Doubtless the constitution of such societies empowers the committees to determine the policy to be pursued, and there would be an end of all authority if it were left optional with the members to accept or not the decision of their committees; yet the very fact that large sums are annually collected by means of fines indicates the frequent resort to compulsion, on every account to be deprecated. On the whole, I cannot help thinking that a more elastic system would operate better, and prove in the end even more efficient than the present stringent method of action.

The principal objects which Trade Unions have in view are the regulation of the supply of labour and the supervision of the rate of wages. By controlling the labour of their own members, by endeavouring to equalize the supply of labour all over the country, by regulating and restricting the admission of apprentices, by hindering the employment of boy and woman labour, and by putting obstacles to the employment of non-unionists, the Trade Societies hope to maintain a monopoly of labour, and thereby to reduce that competition among labourers which is so formidable a barrier to the rise of wages. Nay, more; in the hope of spreading the work among as large a number of members as possible, they prohibit working overtime. But rules such as these contravene some of the first maxims of legal rights, besides being clearly opposed to sound economy. The mutual rights and duties arising from the contract of labour are simple and direct—so much labour for so much reward. The master has a right to employ his labourers or not as he pleases. The labourer may consent to work or not as he likes. What right has either to interfere with the free action of the other in any matter concerning their respective businesses? The objection to overtime is justified by the plea that it is essential for any labourer overburdened with hard work to have time left for instruction and recreation, and that it is a grievous evil to protract labour beyond what nature seems to suggest. But to lay down any general rule, that no man shall labour beyond a certain number of hours on each day, is to deprive the young and strong of the best opportunity they may have of making hay whilst health and vigour last. It seems very philanthropic to limit the work of the over-employed that some work may be left for the unemployed. But it is, I fear, the law of society, that wealth and employment are not equally distributed. Aptitude for labour is not a common gift, and if we neglect the work which Providence places within our reach, it by no means follows that it will be given to those less fortunate than ourselves.

Apart, however, from any legal or social considerations, what are the economic effects of any effort to monopolize or regulate labour? Are they not to cripple production, which in turn must react on wages? Every hour you take from your daily labour is so much deducted from the profits of production, all the fixed capital being to that extent rendered less productive.

The fewer labourers are at work the less will be produced, unless new machinery comes to take their place. Whenever adult labour is employed where boys and women would be sufficient, so much encouragement is given to a waste of forces which will render production less profitable. But can you prevent an increase of labourers in a profitable industry? High wages are certain to be attractive. An agricultural labourer in the receipt of 15*s*. a week will be too glad to apprentice his son to an engineer, in the expectation of getting 30*s*. or 40*s*. a week. And it is against all natural and economic law to attempt to hinder a process so simple and necessary. There is, indeed, a necessary monopoly of talent which we cannot abolish. The few actors, musicians, painters, barristers, and doctors, who may possess learning and skill far excelling those of the masses of their competitors; the few workmen absolutely superior to others in the perfection of their bodily organs, in the dexterity of their hands and motions, and in the skill with which they execute their task, must, of necessity, have a natural monopoly of the work which may be offered. And they are sure to enjoy the benefit of that monopoly in a larger remuneration than is obtained by their competitors, as a fair compensation for services conferred in the work of production. But to pretend to establish any monopoly whereby labourers, strong or weak, skilful or ignorant, shall derive an equal remuneration, and to entertain any expectation that such higher remuneration may be derived from diminished production—these are wild notions, which no true economic principle will sanction.

On the question whether or not Trade Unions can exercise any influence on wages, I am prepared to make some concessions. Wherever wages are in any measure governed by custom, as to some extent in agriculture, a Trade Society may shake off that dull sloth and produce a sudden improvement. Wherever the labourers are in a position so low and dejected as to be under the necessity of working for wages not sufficient to pay for the simple cost of living, as in the case of the needlewomen, a Trade Society may, by granting temporary help with a view to resistance, operate some reform of wages, though with the almost certain result of either lessening production, and so causing a diminution of employment, or of stimulating machinery. Wherever, moreover, the rate of profit is larger than is necessary to provide for the interest of capital, and a legitimate remuneration for the employer's services, a Trade Society may, by a vigilant supervision, operate upon the margin which may exist between the rate of wages and the rate of profits below which all production would cease, and in all probability succeed in securing part of the same for labour, unless defeated either by the competition of labourers among themselves, or by foreign competition. In the former case, however, wages will remain low, though the profits may be high; and in the latter, wages will fall, and the profits decline also, or, at most, remain stationary. Under any circumstance the advantage derived by Trade Unions can only be temporary, for supply and demand are sure to assert their sway. Shake off the custom if you can, and yet if there be seven persons available to one hundred acres, where four are amply sufficient for agricultural purposes, the competition among the seven to get the employment which can only be had by four will be sure to keep wages low. Enhance by artificial combination the wages in any one business, or in any one district, yet, unless that rise is supported by increased savings, and by the substantial accumulation of capital, it will not, it cannot be sustained. But suppose the employer should secure for himself a large amount of profits out of what would be due to the employees, or by keeping wages unduly low, what can he do with such profits but employ them to render them productive? See how it works practically. In 1860, the exports of the produce and manufactures of the United Kingdom were valued at £136,000,000, and the profits assessed to income tax under

Schedule D were declared at £95,000,000. But trade has been very prosperous ever since, and the result has been that in 1874 the amount of profits so assessed to income tax amounted to £197,000,000, showing an increase of £102,000,000, which you may say went all to the masters, since few or no workmen pay income tax. But wait a little. How was that extra amount of profits gained but by increased production? During that period the amount of exports of British produce rose from £136,000,000 in 1860 to £223,000,000 in 1874. And from that increased production workmen got increased wages. Allow that 20 per cent. of the total amount of produce go in wages, and upon the £87,000,000 of extra production for exports only, at least £17,000,000 more per annum must have been divided among labourers in wages. In truth, the excess of profits must in all, or in part, sooner or later find its way among the people, and that is the best possible guarantee for an equitable distribution of profits among employers and employed.

Trade Unions endeavour to operate on wages by fixing the lowest rate and by determining that all their members shall earn at least that low rate. It is not easy, however, to say what the lowest rate of wages should be under any circumstances. You observe the state of the market, that it is buoyant; the number of orders, which appear numerous. You notice a certain amount of eagerness among the employers in pursuing their operations. And as everything seems to denote activity and progress you say wages must rise. But do not misunderstand high prices for large profits, for a high price may be the result of pure speculation, to be soon followed by a great reaction; or the result of increased cost of the raw materials, which may render production even less remunerative. In truth, it is not possible to fix what the wages should be, any more than you can fix what shall be the price of any article or the rate of interest, and any haphazard way of determining what the lowest rate of wages ought to be, apart from what is produced by the relation of supply and demand, must be uncertain and unsatisfactory. It is somewhat discomforting to feel that we can do comparatively so little for ourselves, that we cannot secure a rise, cannot prevent a fall, and must in a manner stand still. Only, depend upon it, economical laws do *not* stand still, and they will operate quite irrespective of our action.

It has been urged by Trade Unionists that they do not demand any uniformity of wages, but that they only fix the rate under which no member of the Union shall work. Give such of them as deserve it as much more as you please, but none shall work for less. What, however, if what you lay down as the minimum, employers should regard as the maximum? Give to the least capable the maximum wages, and what more can the most capable earn? Again, it is said it is to protect labour against the pernicious system of competition by tender, that labourers must insist upon a uniform minimum rate; but on what principle can the labourers make themselves the guardians of the public interests?

Weak as is generally the power of Trade Unions with reference to the determination of the lowest rate of wages, still more doubtful is the possibility of their being able to maintain any uniformity in the wages and earnings of their members. If there be no such thing as uniformity of talent, skill, judgment, strength, vigour, will, or of anything that constitutes and regulates our real power to act upon matter, how can there be such a thing as a uniformity in the value of the part taken by any number of men in the production of any article? There is no such thing as an average ability, for what is an average but an ideal abstract and imaginary medium of an equal distribution of all the inequalities among individuals of a series? We say the average temperature of England is 50° Fahrenheit, but that is made up of constant changes from day to day, varying from 38° to 71°. And so it is with the average life of a man, or the average loss of ships, or the like. The great value of an average rests in the indication it gives of the medium of the range in those variations, but that does not destroy their existence. In matter of labour, though you may form a fair idea of the average strength and capacity of any number of labourers, that does not affect the fact of their possessing some more and some less of those faculties which are required in production, and which constitute the very basis and conditions of the earning of wages. In the engineering trade, the classification of wages with reference to skill must be carried on to a high point, it having been given in evidence before the Royal Commissioners on Trade Unions, that in an establishment of more than 900 men there were as many as 267 rates of wages earned. The introduction of machinery may have reduced the great extremes, many of those feats of force and skill which at one time placed one workman so much above another being now done by machinery. Yet there is room enough left for the display of superior personal ability, strength, and judgment, and to attempt to enforce any ideal uniformity in wages is as unsound in principle as it is mischievous in practice.

Partly with a view to uniformity of wages, and partly also as a means of defence against the masters' attempts to reduce wages, some Trade Societies have resisted what is called payment by piecework. The different systems of payment of wages, by time as by the day or hour, or by piecework as according to results, or by a combination of the two as by time with relation to so much work done, are respectively adapted to different descriptions of labour. For the performance of labour requiring great exactitude and patient attention, payment by time is probably the best. For the performance of work admitting of great swiftness of operation, payment by piecework appears fair for the workman and just to the employer; whilst for the execution of work demanding both precision of execution and economy of time, the combined system seems the best adapted. In any case there can be no doubt that payment by result is the least fallible test of the value of labour, whilst it is the only mode by which patient labour and superior intelligence can raise itself above the surrounding level of low mediocrity. It is alleged against piecework that it incites the worker to work longer hours than is good for him, that it tempts him to hurry over the work, and leave it imperfectly finished; that it is often abused by the master appointing middle men, or piece-masters, to fix the price arbitrarily; that it is used by the master to cut down the wages to the minimum, thus preventing the labourer from deriving any corresponding benefit from his greater labour and exertion. Far be it from me to justify any such practices. I admit that the system may be greatly abused by both masters and workmen. I allow that unprincipled men may use it as a snare, rather than as a fair mode of rewarding labour. And I cannot too strongly condemn any attempt on the part of either to make it the vehicle of fraud and usurpation. But as to the objections that piecework is a system by which the weakest always goes to the wall, or that it incites the labourer to work too much, or that it gives an advantage to the skilful over the unskilful, I fear that, practically hard as such objections may prove in some cases, they are but futile in this matter-of-fact world. A paternal government, be it by societies or by the State, can never be advantageous, and you cannot inflict a deeper injury on any number of people than by taking from them the right to utilize their forces and energies to the maximum of their power. It is the great recommendation of piecework that it is conducive to a better reward of skill, strength, and energy, that it affords the best possible encouragement to improvement in workmanship, and that it is a beneficial instrument to the increase of the productive power of the nation. Some difficulty, however, does doubtless exist in the adoption of the piecework system in different industries. Taking as our guide the two principles already enunciated, that whilst on the one hand the contract of labour is not so many hours in a day, but so much work for so much money; and on the other, that the wages themselves are a commutation of something certain and fixed for the uncertain share which might fall on the workman of the result of production,—it is evident that whilst piecework affords the best test of the real amount of work performed, as a basis for the reward of wages, it still fails in this, that it does not produce that certainty of earning which the workman very justly appreciates. In the cotton manufacture, in printing, and in many other industries, where the work to be done is generally uniform, the value of piecework may be estimated with nearly as much correctness as day-work. But in other industries, especially in engineering works, where each article is different from the other, no such certainty can possibly exist. In the printing and cotton industries, the price of the work is arrived at from extensive experience, by a committee of masters and men. In such engineering works as I have mentioned, the price named is simply what the foreman thinks will be a fair remuneration. To my mind, the method of gauging wages by the actual work done, however technically just, is not always practicable, and to force piecework on unwilling labourers, and to provoke a strike upon that question, is conduct which can scarcely be justified. If masters and men are to work harmoniously, piecework must be held out, wherever there is any doubt on the matter, as an inducement for greater exertion, and not as a hard-and-fast rule for the payment of ordinary wages.

It would be interesting to ascertain how far Trade Unions have proved themselves beneficial to the labouring classes in the matter of wages. During the last twenty years, all prices, salaries, and wages have risen considerably. The salaries of clerks at the Bank of England and in every house of trade, the salaries of assistants in wholesale warehouses and workshops, are all higher. In consideration that the cost of living is dearer, and that a higher standard of living has been introduced, more remuneration has been asked and granted in every occupation. But is not this owing to the immense addition to the supply of the precious metals, the largely increased trade, the enormous augmentation of capital? What else but these circumstances have provided for such increase of wages, prices, and salaries? Trade Unions may have clamoured for higher wages in certain branches of industry. But if masons and carpenters, engineers and ironworkers, protected by Trade Unions, have realized a handsome rise, so have agricultural labourers, and especially domestic servants, realized it without any Trade Unions. Simply left to the tender mercies of the law of supply and demand, a cook and housekeeper who twenty years ago was well paid at £16, now cannot be had for £25 to £30. See what supply and demand do in agricultural labour. Take six purely agricultural counties, such as Devon, Dorset, Wilts, Norfolk, Suffolk, and Cambridge, and six agricultural and industrial counties, such as Cheshire, Lancashire, the West Riding of Yorkshire, Durham, Kent, and Monmouthshire. The average wages of agricultural labourers, and the earnings especially by piece-labour, wherever introduced, have risen everywhere, in consequence of the increasing amount of capital invested in agriculture; but whilst the wages in the purely agricultural counties have risen 15 per cent., those in the agricultural and industrial counties, from the simple competition in the demand for labour, have risen 30 to 40 per cent. Making every allowance for special cases, it is absurd to imagine that Trade Unions have been the main instruments in bringing so much additional wealth into the lap of the working classes. If by constant vigilance on the relation of wages to profits, they have caused, in certain instances, a distribution of any excess at an earlier date than might otherwise have taken place, it is quite possible that the sudden rise of wages consequent upon it may have been as rapidly followed by a reaction. And we well know that frequent oscillations of wages and uncertainty of earnings are more an evil than a boon to the working population. Nor should it be forgotten that an employer, who may have for some time been producing at a loss, has a right to retrieve his position by securing somewhat more liberal profits for a certain period, before he can risk to establish a more equitable level between profits and wages. The employer's object in production is profit, and unless he has a fair prospect of reasonable profits, we cannot expect that he will continue to employ his capital or to engage his services in the business.

Fears have been expressed, that Trade Unions, by harassing the employers with constant demands, by thwarting the operation of supply and demand, and by placing restrictions on the freedom of labour, have discouraged production, and placed the industries of the country in danger of foreign competition. But the statistics of trade do not corroborate any such fear. During recent years production has proceeded at an enormous scale, whether through the extension of mechanical agency and steam-power, which has been enormous, or by the larger adoption of production on a large scale, or by an actual increase of manual labour. Nor is foreign competition more formidable now than ever it was. An increase of exports from £136,000,000 in 1860 to £223,000,000 in 1875, an increase in the quantity of coals produced from 80,000,000 tons in 1860 to 132,000,000 tons in 1875, an increase in the tonnage of shipping belonging to the United Kingdom from 4,600,000 tons to 6,152,000 tons in 1875, are facts which do not indicate that the British workman has been idle during the last fifteen years. And what do we find with respect to the relative increase of the productive power of different countries? Compare the exports of Britain with the exports of other countries, and you will find that British exports have increased fully in proportion to those of other countries. Taking the entire amount of exports of seven principal countries, viz., France, Belgium, Holland, Italy, Austria, the United States, and the United Kingdom in 1860 and 1873, you will see that the proportion of British exports to the whole was 37 per cent. in 1860, and 37 per cent. in 1874. Nor can we take the total exports of such countries as a guide to the great question of danger from foreign competition. Comparing the exports of manufactured goods, such as cotton, linen, silk, woollen, from Britain and France in the years 1861 and 1874, it appears that whilst the exports from the United Kingdom increased at the rate of 64 per cent., the exports from France increased at the rate of 60 per cent. Since then, I am sorry to say, the exports from the United Kingdom have been decreasing; but trade has been depressed in nearly every country,—the necessary reaction from many years of unusual buoyancy.

Trade Unions have been charged with having contributed to the deterioration of the character of British workmen, by making them more quarrelsome, more selfish, and more guided by a spirit of antagonism towards employers than heretofore. But I doubt the truth of such sweeping charges. In so far as Trade Unions are concerned, they doubtless consist mostly of skilled artisans who compare favourably with the great mass of the labouring classes; whilst as societies they manifest a degree of organization and a power of management of no mean order. It must be allowed also that the demonstrations of Trade Unionists, and the conduct of workmen during any strike at the present time, contrast favourably with similar exhibitions in times past. We hear of no incendiarism, no outrage, no riotous assemblage. The practices at Sheffield were utterly disowned by the great body of workmen, and though we still hear of picketing and coercion of different kinds, which the committees of trade societies would do well to repress as acts of true cowardice, I am not prepared to join in the cry that our workmen are worse than other people. In the universal progress of society our workmen have not lagged behind. If they are a little more quarrelsome than we would like them to be, it is because they wish to lift themselves up in the scale of society, and because they see the need of protecting their interests, which were too often heretofore held at nought or trodden under foot.

Upon the action of trade societies on their benefit funds, I have scarcely time to touch. For my part, I deeply regret that the high purposes of a benefit society should be mixed up with the contentious questions of restraints of trade. I can conceive of nothing more important than that money laid aside for sickness and burials, for widows and orphans, should be perfectly secure from danger of being swamped up by any warfare with employers. The best service Trade Unions can render to the labouring population is to inculcate habits of thrift, and to check as far as in them lies the evil of intemperance. Let our Trade Unions abandon the advocacy of theories which are contrary to sound economy. Let them adopt a spirit of harmony and conciliation. Let them cease to make war against capital, which is the necessary handmaid of labour. Let them use only such means as the law permits, and society sanctions, for the protection of the just rights of workmen. Let them lead the mass of labourers in the way of solid progress, and they will render themselves the benefactors of the people, and be acknowledged as the friends and trusted helpers of both capital and labour.

VI.

STRIKES AND LOCK-OUTS.

THAT masters and men engaged in industries of a most complex character, so often disturbed by the introduction of new methods and machinery, having much in common, yet each striving for their own distinct interests, should at times find it difficult to avoid disagreements, is not, after all, a matter to cause much surprise. The marvel rather is, that such conflicts occur so seldom, in comparison with the immense number of employers and employed, and that when they do occur, they exercise, comparatively, so small an influence on the general industry of the country.

What gives to such dissensions any degree of importance is the dire effect they have on the large number of persons thereby affected,—the consequence of the modern organization of labour. A passenger ship has often been compared to a floating village, and so a mill, or a factory, gathers around itself a complete community, every inhabitant of which depends on the uninterrupted progress of the special industry. Let the factory or the iron work be in full activity, and you see hundreds of families rejoicing in plenty, dwelling-houses neatly furnished, tradesmen and artificers all earning sufficient incomes, and if the employer be a Sir Titus Salt, or a Sir Francis Crossley, you will find in such communities the church and the school, reading-rooms and savings-banks, the club, and many other institutions which contribute to the moral and intellectual advancement of the labouring population. But let a dissension occur, and a strike or lock-out be resolved upon, and what a sudden blight falls on the whole prospect, what dejection, what sufferings! Here the full loaf is replaced by the half loaf, there are poverty and sickness, everywhere an idleness which makes one sad.

A strike, or the joint action on the part of a body of workmen or persons employed in any department of business, by which each and all refuse to work except under certain prescribed conditions, often with the means of sustenance, or some approximate equivalent to the loss of wages thereby incurred, provided for by a common fund, is war, which, as Lord Bacon defined, is "the highest trial of right." And a grave responsibility rests on those who resort to such a step on any ground not clearly justifiable, who rush into it before exhausting every means of conciliation, and who are not ready to withdraw from it at any moment when a fair compromise can be effected. That a war may be just, at least in diplomatic language (for I doubt the possibility of the justice or moral lawfulness of an act which carries with it so much carnage and destruction), it must at least be dictated by the necessity of defending absolute rights, and be the very last expedient which a nation can resort to.

> "Force is at best
> A fearful thing e'en in a righteous cause.
> God only helps when man can help no more."

Strikes have arisen for the purpose of securing higher wages, for resisting a fall of wages, for opposing or preventing the introduction of machinery, for obtaining a reduction of the hours of labour, for resisting any addition to the number of apprentices. They have been waged against the employment of non-unionists, against contract work, against piece-work and overtime, or to secure overtime beginning earlier. Only the other day there was a strike in London in consequence of the employment of plasterers to do a kind of work which the bricklayers thought they were themselves entitled to do. And in another case, a printing office lost some of its best members for the sole reason that the masters accepted in their employment one who had not a full certificate of apprenticeship, though as able as any of the rest. By what criterion shall we judge of the justice of such a course where there is no inalienable right to depart from? The labourer has a right to his wages, but the rate of wages is a matter of contract, and depends more on the operation of economic laws than on the will of the master. Where is the right of the labourer to prevent any economy of labour by machinery? On what principle can he oppose the employment of non-unionists? The right to resist, and the rectitude of the cause for which resistance is made, are two distinct things.

An impression seems to exist among our workmen that it is advantageous to them to show that they are in earnest in resisting any attempt on the part of masters to ignore their just rights, and that whether they gain or not the object in view in the particular instance, they are enabled by such resistance to secure better terms for the future. A strike, say they, is the only remedy we have in our own hands. What else can we do? What, if masters, strong as a money power, presuming on our weakness, are found to set aside all considerations of moral duty, to stretch unduly the laws of economic science, and to impose conditions which we cannot accept,—what other course can we pursue but refuse to work at their terms, or, in short, to strike? Against such considerations, however, be mindful, I pray you, to place the immediate sacrifices you thereby inflict on yourselves, the injury you cause to large multitudes who can ill spare any cessation of labour, the disorganization of the industry, the hatred and rancour engendered in your relations with your employers, the chance of failure in the struggle, the want of security as to the maintenance of your success should you be so fortunate as to obtain what you strive for, the loss of wages, the loss and waste of funds the fruit of years of labour and privations, the injury to the nation at large; for remember "that trade is a plant of tender growth, it requires sun and soil and fine seasons to make it thrive and flourish. It will not grow like the palm-tree, which with the more weight and pressure rises the more." Ere you strike, I pray you, count the cost. The present dispute in the cotton trade, for instance, is fraught with danger. Whatever reason there may be for revising the standard list, that is no excuse for a strike, especially in mills where no ground of complaint really exists. Nor have the masters any justification for a general lock-out simply because a few workmen in certain mills have unhappily taken such an objectionable course. I cannot expect that anything I may say will influence materially the progress of the dispute. But, if a word of mine can reach the contending parties, most earnestly would I urge on the workmen on strike, at once to return to their work, on the assurance that a committee from both masters and men will be appointed to inquire into the whole matter and forthwith remove any just ground of complaint. And on the masters I would urge not to commit themselves to joint action in the matter, or to anything like a general lock-out, which would be the cause of so much trouble and misery. Ere you resort to a measure so disastrous as to shut the door of your factories to thousands of innocent labourers, I pray you, I beseech of you, count the cost.

Before a war is finally resorted to among nations, diplomacy generally uses its best endeavours to prevent the sad catastrophe, and certainly no step should be omitted to prevent a strike. The rules of many Trade Unions prescribe that in case of dispute, a deputation of two or more members shall wait on the employer and endeavour to come to an amicable arrangement; that the men shall first reason the matter with their employers; that no strike be resorted to without an attempt having first been made to settle the matter of contention between employers and employed by an amicable negotiation; and that where a grievance exists, the labourers shall, in the first place, solicit their employer or foreman for relief from the same. Now it is only fair to expect from the masters that they should follow a similar course, for I do not think it would be beneath their dignity to descend a little and reason with their workmen on the ground of dispute between them. How much misgiving, how much prejudice would be saved, if masters only condescended to reason with their men, not as so many *hands* in their service, but as *men*, working with and for them! When masters give sudden notice of a reduction of wages, without saying why and under what circumstances, the men are under the necessity of taking an immediate course, and having had no previous consultation, or time to deliberate, they cannot help assuming a position of resistance not easily altered by subsequent action. It is an unfortunate consequence of the present organization of labour, or of production on a large scale, that the employers do not deal with the men individually, and that they are therefore called to act together in a kind of combination. But that should not prevent a full mutual understanding of the matter in question. Only, if a deputation be sent to the masters, let it be composed of the most trusted members in their employment. In the choice of an ambassador, care is always taken to send one whose presence shall be acceptable at the Court to which he is to be accredited, and similar care should be exercised in the selection of those who are to represent the wishes and views of the workmen to their masters. Avoid by all means all causes of irritation at a time when you engage in negotiations requiring for their solution mutual forbearance and mutual sympathy. Whatever be the issue of such direct negotiations, care should be taken to allow time to work its own good influence of better counsel and more ripened judgment. A disposition to strike is incident to the association of working men smarting under a sense of wrong. When large numbers have a common grievance, a spirit of opposition is speedily engendered, and it is well if they have not it in their power to act on the impulse of the moment.

It has been said that Trade Unions encourage workmen to resistance. Doubtless the feeling that they have such societies at their back may render workmen less afraid of the issue, but, on the other hand, an organized society, acting upon rules, must also introduce an increased sense of order, subordination, and reflection. Many of such Unions reserve in their own hands the right of deciding whether a strike should be sanctioned or not. Some of their rules perscribe that no strike shall be considered legal without the consent of the majority of the lodges, to all of whom information of any movement has to be sent; that when a strike for an advance of wages is contemplated by any lodge, the secretary is to report the same to the Central Committee, showing the number that would be out, the number of payable members, the state of trade, and the position of the Society in the neighbourhood; that should an attempt be made unnecessarily to reduce the wages of any of the members, or to increase their hours of labour unjustly, they shall first solicit relief from their employers, and afterwards apply to the president or secretary of their branch, who shall call a committee, or general meeting to inquire into the case; and that should the members of any branch leave their employment without having first obtained the sanction of the Executive Committee, such members shall not be entitled to the allowance provided in case of oppression. Would it not be desirable that the rules of the different Unions on such an important matter should be more uniform than they appear to be? I see no reason why Trade Unions should not operate most favourably in matters of strikes, and when we consider that part of the funds entrusted to them is expended in the maintenance of persons on strike, surely it becomes their interest to reduce the demand for such purposes to the minimum possible.

When a strike has, unhappily, commenced, it is too much to expect the maintenance of much courtesy between the parties, and many are the circumstances which tend to increase the bitterness arising from such a forced suspension of labour. The time when the strike happens is often most inconvenient, for advantage is taken of a brisk trade to insist on a rise of wages, just when the employer is, so to say, at the mercy of the employed. What if the work in operation was contracted for on the basis of existing wages? What if the contractor undertook, under penalties of a heavy character, to complete the work within a limited time? What if the season be towards the close, and the opportunity of fulfilling the engagement fast hastening away? Two persons are engaged in a partnership at will, the condition being that either can retire when he pleases. Can either leave at an inopportune moment, when difficult questions are in suspense, when hazardous contracts are pending? And ought there not to be in the relation between masters and men, as far as is possible and is otherwise applicable, the same sense and practice of equity as we expect between partners in trade? A strike occurs, and in the plenitude of your right you take your tools and go. Can you compel others to follow your course? Can you object to others coming to take your place? You may wish to force your master to make the concession you demand, and you may regret seeing your efforts frustrated by the avidity of others to grasp the chance of employment on any condition; but remember, you have no right to interfere, and if you proceed to violence of any kind, even if it be a slight assault, if you indulge in such threats as will convey to the mind of such other parties that you will bring any form of evil upon them, either in their person, property, or reputation, with the intent of forcing them to act otherwise than you wish, or if you intimidate them by any deed or word which might create fear, or if you molest them or obstruct them in the exercise of their rights,—in either of such cases you commit a wrong which may expose you to criminal proceedings.

A reference to past strikes is not very encouraging as to their good results to workmen. In 1834 the workmen in the Staffordshire potteries struck for an advance of wages, and after fifteen weeks the masters yielded. Elated by their success, however, the men thought they could demand more, and so two years after they struck for a diminution in the hours of labour and a restriction in the number of apprentices. But the masters were not so ready now to make concessions. They united together, and they decided to suspend their manufacture whenever the workmen struck to any master. And the strike was an utter failure, though it cost the men £188,000. What was gained on the previous occasion was more than lost only two years after. In 1853 a great strike took place at Preston for higher wages, which were unconditionally demanded. The masters made some concessions, but these were indignantly refused. So the mills were closed, 18,000 hands were rendered inoperative, and after a lengthened struggle, in which the men spent £100,000, submission became unavoidable. A few strikes have proved successful, but many more have utterly failed. Not many years ago seven distinct strikes took place in Lancashire, every one of them unsuccessful. They involved a loss of employment to 38,000 hands. They lasted a long time—one thirty weeks, another fifty weeks—and together they produced a loss in wages of £757,000 ; and if you add to that sum the profits on capital, and the subscriptions, at ¼ of the wages, the total loss exceeded £1,000,000. In the recent unhappy strike in South Wales nearly 120,000 workers stood out against a reduction of wages, and upwards of £3,000,000 in wages was actually lost in the contest. Did they succeed?

Far from it. They refused to accept a reduction of ten per cent., yet eventually they were compelled by the force of events to re-enter work at a reduction of 12½ per. cent.! Suppose, however, you do succeed in the contest. Remember that you will have to work a long time at the higher wages before you can recover what you have lost by forfeiting the entire amount week by week. Suppose you strike for 5s. more wages, or for 1s. more in every pound. Dr. Watt made a calculation to show in how long a time you will get back what you had before. A week is two per cent. of a working year, or two per cent. of the wage of one year. Let the strike succeed, and you will require 1⅝ year, at the increased rate, to make up for 1 month's wages lost; 3⅓ years to make up for 2 months wages lost; 4⅚ years to make up for 3 months' wages lost; 9⅔ years to make up for 6 months' wages lost; and 20 years to make up for 12 months' wages lost.

Do not think that the money distributed by the Trade Societies during the strike goes to diminish the loss of the persons on strike, for the money so consumed is the saving of former labour, which might go towards further production. It is one of the most unfortunate results of a strike, that funds gained by toil and prudence are expended so fruitlessly in times of forced idleness. During a strike you not only lose what you might otherwise earn, but expend what you had amassed. Nor is the loss confined to the workmen. The employer is certainly as great a sufferer, for a strike may not only rob him of his trade for the time being, but may make him lose the custom which he possesses, and the labour of men of skill well versed in the peculiar work he has on hand, never probably to be replaced, and probably affect also his permanent power to produce as economically as heretofore.

If the strike be for higher wages when the condition of the trade or of the nation cannot bear it, either the community will suffer from the increased cost of the article produced, or else it may cause the introduction of machinery. A strike may have the effect of equalizing wages. An industry badly paid may, by a strike, attract to itself part of the wages which fall to another; but no equalization of wages can possibly be equivalent to the production of capital, which alone can support an increase of wages. If the strike be against the introduction of machinery, it may be the means of the trade being transplanted to other places. It was probably an exaggeration, some years ago, when it was asserted that the frequent strikes of shipwrights on the Thames caused shipbuilding to leave the Thames for the Clyde and the Tyne; the real reason being that iron shipbuilding found a more natural home where iron and coals were immediately available. Yet it is no exaggeration to say that an industry distracted and rendered unproductive in one quarter may take wing and find rest in another. I have, indeed, proved in my previous lecture that up to 1873 at least the trade and industry of England had not suffered from the many disturbances which have taken place,—at least, not to any material extent,—and that foreign competition had not till then gained upon British industry. But what has not yet been may still be. The danger remains, though it may not be imminent.

I doubt the possibility of our ever reaching a time when there shall be no strikes, for just in proportion as our labouring population rises to the consciousness of its power, and seeks to participate in a higher degree in the profits of production, so the struggle between capital and labour may be expected to be more frequent. But may we not expect that, side by side with this, a greater disposition may also be engendered to remove sources of quarrel, to soften their asperity when they do arise, and to settle disputes by arbitration and conciliation? Must force ever reign? Is the arbitrament of the sword befitting our character and position in life. The legislature has done whatever it could possibly do to provide for the adoption of more peaceful means. A refusal to leave a matter of dispute to arbitration betokens either haughtiness and arrogance, or weakness. I do not think that the appointment of one or more strangers as arbitrators, be they lords, lawyers, or philanthropists, is a desirable method, for their decision can, at best, be a simple compromise of the immediate ground of dispute; it will never be able to regulate the subsequent action of the parties, and will be certain to leave one of the contending parties dissatisfied with the result. A conciliation board, on the other hand, within the establishment itself, composed of an equal number of masters and men, with a neutral umpire, all of them having a perfect acquaintance, not only with the case in point, but with the bearing of the question generally upon production, and upon the comfort of working as concerning both masters and men, and each of them possessing the full confidence of the parties interested, is sure to give a verdict entitled to respect and assent. But let it be fully remembered that it is the essence of arbitration or conciliation that you commit the matter in dispute to the decision of other parties, and that you thereby incur an obligation to abide by their verdict, whether it may go in your favour or against you,—provided, of course, the arbitrators or the board confine themselves strictly to the matter submitted to them. How far any national board of arbitration may be advantageously established, seems to me very doubtful. The first essential to success in any effort for the prevention of disputes, or their early settlement, is the possession of a conciliatory spirit, and a ready disposition to consider the rights and interests of both sides. Let that spirit prevail within the establishment among both masters and men, and there will be no difficulty in arriving at an equitable and satisfactory settlement of any disputes, however formidable they may appear.

VII.

BUDGETS OF THE WORKING CLASSES.

ABOUT twenty years ago, a work was published in France, by M. Le Play, the superintendent of the Paris International Exhibition, entitled " Studies on the Labour, the Domestic Life, and the Moral Condition of the Working Population of Europe," giving accurate and minute details, from actual fact, of all the money received and expended during one year, by a certain number of families of the working population in every country in Europe; the income including the wages of the head of the family, as well as of the mother and children, counting the actual number of days they were at work, as well as any income from a garden or parcel of land, rent of house or field, produce of pasture, pig, sheep, or from any pension, funds, interest, and any miscellaneous or accidental sources; the expenditure divided into expenses for food and drink, for house, fire, and light, for clothing, for moral, educational, or religious purposes, for taxes, recreation, or debt. And most interesting it is to compare the habits of the different people, and the effects of temperature, climate, race, and religion, on the description and quantity of food and drink used, the nature of their amusements, and the amount devoted to the cause of charity and beneficence. I imagine, however, that if a similar work were attempted regarding the various classes of labourers in England, if, instead of comparing the French and the Russian, the German and the Italian, the Spanish, Turkish, and Greek labourers, with the English, the Scotch, and the Irish, we had before us the real income and expenditure of any number of families in England from among the agricultural, the manufacturing, and the industrial classes, in town and country, and in the metropolis, we would find the same diversity of results, the same strange anomalies, and the same gulf in the different traits of manner and character, as can be found among them in any part of the world.

How, then, can I venture to give you the budgets of the working classes? Of what guidance can the income and expenditure of one family of five be to the income and expenditure of another family of ten? What is there in common between a bachelor living in lodgings and a young couple with two babies, and it may be with a mother or father to keep? The ways of life are very different; so much depends on the surroundings of the family, on the mode in which the parties have been brought up, the character, the education, the state of health, and a vast variety of circumstances, that, really, every household is a world of itself. Home is the Englishman's castle—impregnable and inaccessible; who can assail it? No; my object is not to pry into matters which are happily beyond the public gaze, but rather to lay before you the value and importance of simply taking a good account of what we are actually receiving, and what we are actually spending, during the whole of a long year. You are aware that one of the most important evenings of the Session in Parliament is the evening when the Chancellor of the Exchequer makes his financial statement; that is, when he reviews all the circumstances connected with the income and expenditure of the State during the preceding year, investigates the condition and prospects of the nation as respects the future, communicates his calculations of the probable income and expenditure for the year to come, and declares whether the burthens upon the people are to be increased or diminished. This statement is familiarly known as the Budget, and it is regarded with the greatest possible interest by the whole nation. Now if this is a good practice for the State, would it not be an excellent practice for private individuals also! The large questions that have engaged our attention in the previous lectures are most important. A knowledge of the economic laws which govern the rate of wages is most interesting and valuable. Still more important, however, in any case, is it to come home to ourselves, and to consider whether our own annual income is fully equal to our expenditure, whether every item of income of every member of the family is duly gathered, accounted for, and properly utilized, and whether the expenditure is, in every respect, moderate, legitimate, and kept within proper control. " Gear is easier got than guided." Have you ever tried to keep a diary? The difficulty of persevering in it is immense. You require habits of order and method not often possessed. Carefully to note down what we are doing, and what happens to us every day, is as difficult as to register all the money that comes and goes. Merchants, who make all their payments by cheques, and who draw all their current money by cheques on their bankers, have a ready means of ascertaining what they get and expend during the year. But those who have not the luxury of a banker must keep a little book for themselves; and it is wonderful how useful and interesting it becomes in course of time for a comparison with the past and a check for the future. Let your wife begin to put down what she expends, and you begin to put down what you expend,—and what a monitor such a record will prove!

The pay of the labourer is his wages, but his earnings will comprise also the produce of labour from any other industry at spare hours, any allowance from any society, and the fruit of any money or property he or any member of his family may have at the savings bank, building society, trade society, or otherwise. The pay itself may consist either in money or in kind, or in both; and where clothing, board, or lodging is given, the money value of the same ought to be taken into account. A sailor who gets 60*s.*, or 70*s.*, and sometimes 90*s.*, per month, must remember that during the whole time of his engagement he is fed and lodged on board. An agricultural labourer often gets very little money wages. But in Northumberland the wages include an allowance of corn for a cow or pig, house and garden, coals, etc. A hind's poll in Scotland comprises a given quantity of oats, barley, peas, and land enough for potato planting. In Devonshire, besides the money wage, there is the allowance of cider, and a labourer has a cottage for £2, with a patch of land, from which he can get vegetables for the whole year for the entire family, and enough to feed a pig, which again becomes a source of income. A domestic servant gets from £10 to £30 a year, in money, besides board and lodging, which, in London at least, are equivalent to as much again. In the occupations I have noted, the combination of payment in money and kind is not only indispensable, but really advantageous to the labourers. In calculating the amount of earnings, therefore, do not forget the value of the advantages you obtain from your employment over and above the weekly or monthly wages in money.

Where, moreover, there are more earners than one in a family, where the wife, or sons, or daughters, earn also money, and bring it into the common purse, that must be calculated also.¹ I imagine sons and daughters do not bring to their fathers and mothers all they earn, or anything like it. Would that they did! A very large portion of the earnings of the younger members of the whole working population is, I fear, utterly wasted, simply because it never reaches the home treasury. The practice of either father or children allotting any portion of their wages to the wife or mother for their food, keeping the rest for themselves, and throwing on the poor mother the burden of making the two ends meet, is wrong in principle. The boarding system is wrong when applied to the family. Oh for a return to the patriarchal system of united and not divided interest! There are thousands of families of working people in England where the aggregate earnings would amount to £3 or £4 a week, but where no account is taken of a great portion of the same. I am not exaggerating when I say that in very many cases fully one-fourth of the income of the family is, in this way, utterly squandered, leading to no result, giving no comfort, and only going in waste, drunkenness, and vice. It is the same, unfortunately, in the country as in towns. The agricultural villages, which have been greatly multiplied since the introduction of machinery into agriculture, are the absorbent of most of the earnings of many hard-working agricultural labourers. The public-house, the music hall, and other places of amusement, waste away many an income which could maintain a family in honour and comfort.

In order to make the income and the expenditure meet, there are only two ways: one is, to increase the income; the other is, to diminish the expenditure. Don't you be deceived into any expectation that you may increase your income by any other means than by hard work. Don't you be so foolish as to renounce any income now in the hope that by renouncing it to-day, you may get more to-morrow. Get what you can, and keep what you have, is the way to get rich. Don't you trifle with any penny you may get, simply trusting on the continuance of health and work to earn more. Trust in Providence? Yes, but never forget the duty of using rightful means. There is one source of income, moreover, which we should scorn to resort to, unless under the direst necessity, and that is, the poor rate. I am strongly of opinion that the poor law in England is most destructive to the industry, forethought, and honesty of the labourers. What more degrading than using the parish doctor both for birth and death? What more lowering than the workhouse? What more inconsistent with political economy than the supporting, by public rates, of able-bodied labourers? It is a noble axiom, that none shall die of hunger,—that the wealth of the rich shall supply the necessities of the poor. But it is communistic in essence, and in practice most mischievous. The subject is a very difficult one, and a change from a system which has been so long in use might be attended with hardship; but it is for the working classes to say how long a compulsory charity shall be allowed to enervate the very vitals of their character and independence. They manage poor relief better in other countries. In Sweden, every able-bodied person is expected to maintain himself, his wife, and children, as a legal obligation. In France, there is no legal claim for support. "When the virtue of charity ceases to be private," said M. Thiers, "and becomes collective, it ceases to be a virtue, and it becomes a dangerous compulsion." In Belgium, the classic land of pauperism, there is no poor rate. The legal provision for the support of the poor consists in the donations of the public, vested in, and administered by, the civil authorities. In Elberfeld there is a right to relief, but outdoor relief is entrusted to overseers, and every person applying for help must show that he cannot exist without it. In Italy there is no legal provision for the support of the poor. Comparing the proportion of pauperism to population, England may seem to stand better than any other country; but remember, the amount of charity in England, over and beyond any provision of the poor law, is far in excess of what is given abroad. Look at the report of the Charity Commissioners. See how much is spent and squandered in every parish. See what is passing through the poor box in every police office in the metropolis. The public support of the sick, the lame, the blind, the old, and the helpless infant, is a duty; but it is a disgrace in any one who earns enough and, it may be, to spare, to abandon an old father or mother, a wife or a child, to the miserable pittance of the parish. It is a shame and a crime, by extravagance and waste, to throw our burden off our shoulders. Burden, did I say? There is no sweeter joy, no pleasanter duty, than to contribute to the well-being of our dear ones, our friends, and our kindred.

It is time, however, to turn to the other side of the account—the expenditure. There is a well-known saying fitly applicable to our subject—"Cut your coat according to your cloth." Measure your expenditure by your income. It is a most unfortunate practice of our Chancellor of the Exchequer, in making up the financial statement of the nation, that he does exactly the reverse, by measuring the public income by the public expenditure. But he can do that, because he has a whole nation to fall upon, by compulsory taxation. Not so the private individual. You and I have no other resource than what we earn; and we must, of necessity, measure our expenditure by that, and by nothing else whatever. In any case, under no circumstances, allow yourselves to fall into debt, for it is the certain source of ruin. "Out of debt out of danger." A very large number of the plaints brought before the county courts consist of sums not exceeding 40*s.*, and many are for sums not exceeding 1*s.* It is impossible to exaggerate the burden, the aggravation, the misery, and the dependence of a man who gets into the habit of purchasing what he requires, often, it may be, in excess of what he needs, but with the consciousness of not having the wherewithal to pay for it. "Cut your coat according to your cloth." Never give out what does not come in. Avoid, above all, shop debt; for you pay very dear for it, in exorbitant prices of all you purchase. I do hope Mr. Bass will succeed in his effort to abolish imprisonment for debt, as a discouragement to shops to sell on credit, for then prices would sink to the scale of cash prices, and shopkeepers would get rid of a great deal of care. Have the money before you spend it, and you will be sure to economise it to the very best.

> "Ken when to spend, and when to spare,
> And when to buy, and you'll ne'er be bare."

The expenditure of a working man's family cannot differ very much from the expenditure of a person of the middle classes, except in this, that the proportion of what is spent in necessaries, comforts, or luxuries must vary according to the amount of income. With 50*s.* or 60*s.* a week, you may devote some portion to the comforts or even the luxuries of life. With 20*s.* a week, you may be thankful if you can provide for the necessaries of life. Our absolute wants usually consist of bread, flour, vegetables, meat, butter, sugar, tea, and milk; house-rent, fire and light, clothing, and the education of children. These are the necessaries of life. The comforts of life consist, probably, in an extensive use of these very things, plus spices and condiments, newspaper and omnibus, church and charity, an excursion, and some insurance for the future. And the luxuries may consist of tobacco and drink, frivolities, pots of flowers, keeping of birds, etc. But are we all agreed in such a classification as this? Time was when white bread was a luxury; now it is an article of common use, as a necessary of life. Meat is necessary, but is it necessary to eat it every day? And is there not a material difference between purchasing a prime joint and other portions equally if not more nutritious? Clothing is necessary, but what clothing? Are bonnets with feathers and flowers necessary? Are twenty yards necessary for a dress? Need we all dress in silk attire? Whether an article of use is to be classed among the necessaries, comforts, or luxuries of life depends in a great measure on the standard by which we are guided, on the ideal we form for ourselves of our own wants.

Looking over a large number of budgets in the work already quoted on European labourers, in returns kindly sent to me direct by several workmen, and in the reports of the Secretaries of Legation on the industrial condition of the working classes abroad,[*] the conclusion I arrive at of a legitimate appropriation of wages is somewhat as follows : 60 per cent.

---

[*] See Appendix B.

is required for food and drink; 12 per cent. for rent and taxes; 10 per cent. for clothing; 6 per cent. for fire and light; 1 per cent. for newspapers, omnibus, or travelling; 4 per cent. for church, education, and charity; 2 per cent. for amusements; and 5 per cent. for savings. In other words, for every pound of wages the expense would be—12s. for food and drink; 2s. 6d. for lodging; 5d. for firing and light; 2s. for clothing; 2d. for omnibus and newspaper; 1s. 6d. for church, education, and charity; 5d. for amusements; and 1s. for saving in any insurance company or benefit club. But this takes no account of the doctor's bill, nor of slack time, and it would be only fair that some economy should be made in either of the items to meet these possible, if not unavoidable, drawbacks. Nor are drink and tobacco specially calculated, for the cost of a reasonable quantity of beer should certainly be included in the 12s. for food and drink, and the cost of the tobacco should be included in the expense for amusement,—if, by any construction of language, smoking can be considered an amusement. As a general rule, the necessaries of life should be first provided; and whatever excess may remain may go towards the comforts of life; but, under any circumstance, leave something for saving. It may be kind to be liberal, and to be anxious to make every member of the family, day by day, as comfortable as your means allow; but it is kinder far to provide something for the almost inevitable contingency of sickness, want of work, or old age, when you, that are now the strength and support of the family, are compelled sadly to put all work aside, or when any member of your family, from disease or otherwise, may have to draw more on your resources than you are able to provide.

Need I say that a considerable economy may be effected in our every-day expenditure without abridging in the slightest manner our means of subsistence and comfort? You buy $\frac{1}{4}$ of an ounce of the best tea, and you are charged $\frac{3}{4}d.$—equivalent to 4s. per pound. Buy $\frac{1}{2}$ pound for cash, and you may get the same tea at the rate of 3s. or 2s. 6d. per pound. Is there not much waste in our cooking? Is there not wanton waste in many of our household arrangements? A penny here and a penny there, and soon shillings and pounds vanish. It is, however, impossible, when we come to details such as these, not to place in the very foremost rank of waste a very considerable portion of what is spent in drink. Am I wrong in supposing that a person earning 30s. a week will spend 3s. in drink, that being considered a moderate allowance for dinner and supper? Am I exaggerating when I say that in a very large number of cases that proportion is far, far exceeded, the amount so expended often being more than 25 or 30 per cent. of the income? What is the use of reasoning on economy in little matters with such a drain as this? What can the poor wife do with the very small amount entrusted to her for housekeeping? And how often does a dissipated husband make a dissipated wife! What a wretched example for children! What a source of vice and crime drunkenness is proving over the whole country! I am not in favour of the so-called Permissive Bill, because it would introduce strife in parishes, and because I think it would, at best, be of partial application, and might be applied just where it is least needed. Nor can I say that we should lightly interfere with any legitimate business, or with the common rights of the people. If there is a demand, the supply will most assuredly be forthcoming somehow or other. No, the reform must begin with ourselves. Reasons of duty, reasons of self-respect, reasons of education, must impel us to remove this source of scandal, at any rate, from our own shoulder, and by our exhortation, and by our example, strive to blot it out from the escutcheon of England. When I last visited Liverpool I was attracted by the cocoa-shops established in the immediate centre of the dock and sea-faring population, and there I got a mug of cocoa for $\frac{1}{2}d.$ and a scone for $\frac{1}{2}d.$—both excellent and satisfying. Take that in the morning, and you will find it an excellent preservative against any craving for strong drink. All honour to Mr. Lockhart for his noble efforts in that direction. Would that we had such cocoa-shops in London! Would that public-houses without drink, and public coffee and working men's clubs, were multiplied, for I am sure there is ample room, and an imperious need, for extensive efforts in improving the morals of the people in this one direction. I do not trust much in the power of an Act of Parliament to make people temperate. But I do trust in a sound and wholesome public opinion, and I appeal to you to create it by your hearty, spontaneous, and energetic example and action. Who will help in this glorious enterprise? Do not wait for great opportunities. Begin at once, and at home. In Mr. Smiles' excellent work on Thrift there is a story illustrative of the influence of example in this matter which is worth repeating :—

"A calico printer in Manchester was persuaded by his wife, on their wedding-day, to allow her two half-pints of ale a day, as her share. He rather winced at the bargain, for, though a drinker himself, he would have preferred a perfectly sober wife. They both worked hard, and he, poor man, was seldom out of the public-house as soon as the factory was closed. She had her daily pint, and he, perhaps, had his two or three quarts, and neither interfered with the other, except that, at odd times, she succeeded, by dint of one little gentle artifice or another, to win him home an hour or two earlier at night, and now and then to spend an entire evening in his own home. They had been married a year, and on the morning of their wedding anniversary the husband looked askance at her neat and comely person, with some shade of remorse, as he said, 'Mary, we've had no holiday since we were wed ; and, only that I have not a penny in the world, we'd take a jaunt down to the village to see thee mother.'

"'Would'st like to go, John?' said she, softly, between a smile and a tear, so glad to hear him speak so kindly,—so like old times. 'If thee'd like to go, John, I'll stand treat.'

"'Thou stand treat!' said he, with half a sneer: 'has't got a fortune, wench?'

"'Nay,' said she, 'but I've gotten the pint o' ale.'

"'Gotten what?' said he.

"'The pint o' ale,' said she.

"John still didn't understand her, till the faithful creature reached down an old stocking from under a loose brick up the chimney, and counted over her daily pint of ale, in the shape of three hundred and sixty-five threepences, or £4 4s. 6d., and put them into his hand, exclaiming, 'Thou shalt have thee holiday, John!'

"John was ashamed, astonished, conscience-stricken, charmed, and wouldn't touch it. 'Hasn't thee had thy share? Then I'll ha' no more!' he said. He kept his word. They kept their wedding day with mother, and the wife's little capital was the nucleus of a series of frugal investments, that ultimately swelled out into a shop, a factory, a warehouse, a country seat, a carriage, and perhaps a Liverpool mayor."

In England, the working classes have not much reason to complain that their taxes are too heavy. That every subject of the kingdom should, in proportion to his means, contribute his quota to the general taxation is a principle of finance universally admitted. As members of the commonwealth, we are all, though certainly in different degrees, interested in securing its preservation and advancement. The poorest among us feels an interest, if not pride, in the honour and glory of his fatherland. In truth, we should regard the national expenditure in the light of an insurance, and the payment of the premuim as a common duty and privilege. During the last thirty years, however, nearly every step in the reform of the Budget has been in the direction of lessening the taxes which pressed on the necessaries of life, and of increasing the taxes affecting wealth, industries, and, especially, luxuries. Taxes on sugar, tea, coffee, corn, and on a vast number of imported articles have been greatly reduced, or remitted altogether; and in their stead, stamp duties, income tax, land tax, probate duties, and duties on spirits, malt, wine, and tobacco have been newly imposed or increased. And what is the result? Of the taxes affecting wealth and industry, amounting in all to £23,000,000, the working classes do not pay more than half a million. Of taxes on necessaries they may pay probably £2,500,000—the greater part on tea. But of the taxes on luxuries, including spirits, malt, and tobacco, the working classes pay their full quota in some £23,000,000 a year. But this large sum of taxation, borne by the working classes under this head, is entirely voluntary. Give up drinking, give up tobacco, and you avoid nearly every farthing of taxation. Nowhere, probably, are the working classes treated with more consideration than in England. What a pity that greater advantage is not taken of this wonderful exemption! As it is, no tax of any consequence is paid by the working classes, except in the slight addition caused by the duties on the cost of their spirits, malt liquor, or narcotics; and no one would grumble if these taxes were considerably increased.

I have ventured to give what might be deemed a legitimate distribution of the expenditure of our working classes. Now, look at the results. I have estimated the total annual wages and earnings of the working classes at the large amount of £400,000,000, including money and money's worth; but take no account of money's worth, and assume only £300,000,000 in hard cash as falling into the hands of our working classes. And on the proportion given, the money should go in the following shapes: £180,000,000 would be expended on food and drink; £36,000,000 in rent; £6,000,000 in firing and light; £30,000,000 in clothing; £3,000,000 in newspapers, omnibuses, and railway travelling; £12,000,000 in church, education, and charity; £6,000,000 in amusements; whilst £15,000,000 would be reserved for savings. But is the money so expended? Let us see. We may fairly assume that the £180,000,000 is fully expended in food. The £36,000,000 laid down for house-rent tallies, so far, with the census report of 1871, showing that the rental of houses under £20 had an estimated aggregate annual value of £32,000,000. Fire and light will cost quite as much as I have estimated. The amount given for clothing is, I fear, rather below than above the amount annually expended. And so, probably, the amount given for amusements and other items. But as for the £12,000,000 expended in church, education, and charity, and £15,000,000 reserved for saving, alas! where are they? No, my calculations are fallacious in two distinct items. Instead of the 60 per cent. given for food covering the amount expended in drink, that item, to the extent of fully 15 per cent. of the whole income, or £45,000,000, and also 2 per cent. or £6,000,000 for tobacco, or, in all, £51,000,000, must be added as a separate and additional expenditure. But if this large amount is really so expended, as is, unhappily, most likely to be the fact, if it is not indeed greatly exceeded, what remains for church, education, and charity, or for savings, or for any other rational purpose? Positively nothing. The little saved—probably £3,000,000 or £4,000,000 a year—as indicated in the annual increase of the amount in the savings banks, friendly and building societies, co-operative societies, etc., is the fruit of the economies of some families, too few in number to constitute any perceptible percentage in the whole number of the working population of the country.

Now this I consider a very lamentable result of the budgets of the working classes. What wonder if debt and pauperism be rampant? What surprise can it cause that days of sunshine and prosperity are so soon followed by dark, dark days of misery and wretchedness? I hope I may be wrong in my calculations. But if I am not, as I fear is not the case, it may not be in vain that I have called your attention to the subject. In discoursing upon the budgets of the working classes, it would be wrong to ignore the thousand cases of real, unmistakable hardship. That there is real poverty in the land, that there is suffering, want, and misadventure, who can ignore? The difficulties of the poor, their valour and fortitude in bearing with and mastering them, are best known to those who come most intimately in contact with them. Their charitable disposition towards their friends in trouble, their self-sacrifice, their heroism in labour, have been depicted by the most masterly hands. But I am now speaking to the great mass of our working men and women, and I say, if you will avoid falling into the deep mire of calamities, if you will maintain yourselves in comfort, honour, and self-reliance, look to your budget, and endeavour so to economise your income that you may have always enough and to spare.

VIII.

SAVINGS BANKS AND OTHER INVESTMENTS OF THE WORKING CLASSES.

THE drift of all my Lectures has been—Look well into your estate. Large economies depend upon little economies. If you must be liberal in some kind of expense, do try to save in some other. If you will be plentiful in diet, be at least saving in drink. Let not your candle burn at both ends. By all means, try to save. But how? By putting aside whatever is not absolutely indispensable for present want, in order that you may make a reserve for unforeseen eventualities. And be not ashamed to save. Call it not penury, miserliness, niggardliness, and the like. A disposition to save for the future, a prescience of, and a preparation for, what is to come, are just what place us above the brute. Savages are not thrifty. They live from day to day. It is prudence that prompts us to save, and wisdom that regulates the amount of our savings. It is moderation which enables us to realize any saving, and intelligence which enables us to render it fruitful. And what are prudence, wisdom, moderation, and intelligence, but the offspring of civilization and morals? To have no thought for the morrow, to have no regard for the welfare of friends and relatives, to make no provision for old age and sickness, to indulge in waste while the sun shines, never reflecting that after summer comes winter, are not consistent with our moral duties and obligations. Is it a true picture of the English what Mr. Smiles said, that though they are a diligent, hard-working, and generally self-reliant race, they are not yet sufficiently educated to be temperate, provident, and foreseeing; that they live for the present, and are too regardless of the coming time; that, though industrious, they are improvident—though money-making, they are spendthrift. I would fain believe that the future is too highly drawn, for, certainly, there is no nation of the world that puts aside so much wealth from year to year as England. What is it but thrift that renders this country able to accumulate capital at such an enormous ratio? Ask the merchant and the manufacturer, and they will tell you that they must and do strain every nerve to increase their capital. The State, it is true, has no reserve in the Tower to meet any possible contingency of war as France had, prior to the Napoleonic wars, in the palace of the Tuileries. We make no account of the blessing of water when it rains in abundance. We have no public granaries for the storing of the surplus of prosperous harvest years. Yet production and saving must be far in excess of our expenditure, or else how could wealth increase so fast? No, there is much saving going on in England, but the effort is made comparatively by the few. How often do we see calculations, almost fabulous, of what good could be done if we would only put aside what is superfluous or wasteful! What number of churches and schools, of museums and palaces, of parks and gardens, could be built and provided with the expenses now allotted to the army and navy, or the sum devoted to the interest of the national debt, or the amount expended in drink, or any other luxuries. Alas! alas! the dreams of the reformer are not so easily realized.

The first step in the way of saving is to spend well. You save one pound. Spend it on some evening classes to learn drawing or mechanics, arithmetic or French, whatever may be most useful to you. Remember, we are never too old to learn. Better late than never. You save another pound. Buy Cassell's Popular or Technical Educator. Spend it in, or set it aside towards, a new set of tools for your employment. Lay it out, in short, in what may be useful to you in improving your fitness for work, in enabling you to raise yourself and earn better wages. How much has been set aside in tools and implements by our working classes it would be difficult to estimate. A joiner's tools may be worth £10, and more, but unhappily with the introduction of machinery the labourer is no longer called to provide himself with tools and implements, and so this form of saving is rather diminishing than increasing. Well prepared for your work, look to your house. By all means let it be comfortable, cheerful, and well furnished. Mr. Mundella noticed the great demand for pianofortes and other musical instruments for working men's houses. Do not indulge in luxuries, but do take a pride in having a pretty house, a full house, and a comfortable home. Am I wrong in taking £10 each, at least, as the value of furniture in the 3,500,000 houses tenanted by working people? If so, then some £35,000,000 or £40,000,000 must have been set aside by them in this form.

Under no circumstances, I pray you, keep your money in your pockets, for it may not be long there. The coin is round, and it rolls away swiftly. Temptations are strong. The shops are inviting. If you keep your money loose, you may not have the fortitude to resist the attraction to spend it amiss. So put it aside. And where? Not inside an old stocking, not under a brick, but at the savings bank. The savings banks only commenced with the opening of the present century. In 1798, a Miss Priscilla Wakefield founded a bank at Tottenham, for receiving the savings of workwomen and female domestic servants. In 1799, an offer was made by the Rev. Joseph Smith, of Wendover, to receive any part of the savings of the people in his parish every Sunday evening, during the summer, and to repay them at Christmas, with the addition of one-third of the whole amount deposited, as a bounty; and in 1810, the Rev. Henry Duncan founded the Parish Bank Friendly Society at Ruthwell. These were the days of small things, but institutions of this nature soon multiplied, and so a Bill was introduced in the House of Commons by Mr. Whitbread to make use of the Post Office machinery for the purpose of receiving and repaying the savings of the people, though matters were not ripe for that step. However, in 1817 the first Act was passed upon the subject, authorising the formation of savings banks for the purpose of receiving deposits of money for the benefit of the persons depositing, allowing the same to accumulate at compound interest, and to return the whole, or any part of the same, to depositors, after deducting the necessary expense of management, but deriving no profit from the transaction. The limit of the deposits was set at £100 for the first year, and £50 for every year following, and the interest allowed to depositors was 4 per cent. net; the Commissioners for the Reduction of the National Debt paying the trustees for the amount invested with them, at the rate of 3d. per day for every £100, producing an interest of £4 11s. 3d. Some change was made in the limits of deposits in 1824, reducing it to £30 for the first year, and £30 for the subsequent ones; the whole not to exceed £150, and interest to cease when principal and interest amounted to £200,—as at present. But money having become less valuable, in 1844 the interest to depositors was reduced to £3 0s. 10d. per cent. per annum. And how great has been the success of such measures! In 1817, on the first formation of these banks, the amount due to depositors was £231,000. In 1831, the amount rose to £15,000,000, and thirty years after, in 1861, it reached £42,000,000. By that time, however, the proposal to make use of the Post Office for facilitating the employment of the savings of the people acquired more force from the failure of some savings banks, whilst the eagerness shown by the people in France in responding to the appeal of Napoleon III. for one loan after another, with full confidence in their national securities, commended the use of the Post Office as an instrument for multiplying the means of depositing the savings of the people all over the country, as alike convenient and advantageous. So the suggestion years before made by Mr. Whitbread was taken up in earnest. And in 1860 Mr. Gladstone laid before the House of Commons a plan which became the basis of the present system. For a short time, the old savings banks somewhat suffered from the presence of these fresh competitors, but they speedily recovered, and now whilst the Trustees Savings Banks have an amount as large as ever, or £42,000,000, the Post Office Banks, so suddenly sprung up, have already in hand £25,000,000—making in all £67,000,000.

This amount is supposed to represent, at least to a large extent, the savings of the labouring classes. There is no means, however, of ascertaining the classes of persons to whom such deposits really belong. The probability is that not an inconsiderable portion of such savings belongs to the middle classes, who need such instruments of saving quite as much as the working classes. If we take two-thirds of the whole amount as belonging to the working classes, the sum to their credit would be £45,000,000. Nor is this all, for there are a large multitude of small savings banks connected with Sunday schools, churches, and other societies, which are of great value, and which would be found to have together a handsome sum. The present Post Office Savings Banks fail in their not being open in the evening, particularly on Fridays and Saturdays, in their not receiving less than one shilling at a time, and in their limiting the deposits to £30 a year. The Society of Arts and the Provident Knowledge Society represented these wants to the Postmaster-General, and whilst he consented to open the banks in the evening, at least gradually, he objected to the diminution of deposits to less than 1s. on the ground of expense.

As it is, every transaction of a depositor, whether he pays in or draws out money, costs the State nearly 6*d*. Let the deposit be 1*d*., and for each transaction the cost may be 1*s*. To the objection against the limits of £30, the Postmaster said that it was necessary to maintain it on account of expense, and also for the purpose of keeping clear of competition with the ordinary business of bankers. Meanwhile, however, the National Penny Bank has been founded, in which our friend Mr. Hamilton Hoare takes a deep interest. It is open in the evening. It has school branches and workshop branches, and it is perfectly safe. Patronise it with your pennies. Do not imagine, indeed, that every penny or pound once deposited at the savings banks is allowed to remain there. Far, far from it. It is an advantage certainly of the savings bank that you have no trouble in taking out whatever you need, but remember the pith and marrow of the transaction is to keep the money there. Once taken out, unless, indeed, for the purpose of a better investment, and it is done. Look at the accounts for 1875, for England only. During that year the old Trustees Savings Bank received £6,656,000, and actually paid out £7,049,000, or more than they got. True, some of that money has possibly been transferred to the Post Office Savings Banks, and there we find that they received in the year £8,779,000, and paid back £6,864,000. But, certainly, it is not satisfactory that, with receipts amounting in all to upwards of £15,000,000, the amount left, or saved, in all the savings banks in one year, was only £1,522,000. Just imagine how many must have tried to save something, and how few have been able to manage it. How many must have started with a good resolution, how few were strong enough to keep to it. And how many must have used the savings banks simply for a temporary convenience, probably till Christmas or Whitsuntide, or till the want or the fancy came to buy something. Thankful, indeed, we may be that so much has been gathered, and that such a substantial sum as £45,000,000, or thereabout, remains there on account of the working classes. Only remember, it is the accumulation of very many years. As a matter of fact, if we compare the deposits per head of the population in 1851 and 1874, we find that the smallest per centage increase has been in England. Whilst in England the increase was at the rate of 53 per cent., in Ireland it was 175 per cent., and in Scotland 200 per cent.

In connection with savings banks I pray you to remember that by allowing 3 per cent. per annum the nation loses a large sum of money every year.* The Post Office Savings Banks allow only 2½ per cent., and I venture to say that with the present low value of money it will not be long before the Trustees Savings Banks will have to revise their system, unless they obtain greater freedom in the choice of investments. In France, the savings banks invest their funds in landed and other real property, as well as in the public funds. In Belgium, they even discount bills. In Holland, they lend on mortgages. Need I say that in the United Kingdom all the deposits are invested in the British funds? Whether or not greater latitude might be allowed in the investments consistently with sufficient security, is a question for grave consideration. Comparing the savings bank system in England and other countries, it would appear that England stands far ahead, in Europe at least. In 1874, in England and Wales, the savings banks had £2 7s. 8d. per head, Scotland £1 11s. 1d., Ireland 11s., France 9s. 10d., Holland 5s. 4d., Austria 36s. 4d., Germany 37s., Switzerland 84s., Italy 16s. 6d. While Great Britain had 9,426 depositors for every 100,000 persons, Switzerland had 20,312, and France only 5,600. But, for purposes of comparison, you must take into account other facilities of investments, and the habits of the people. The working people of France and Belgium are less venturesome than those of England.

* On the 20th November, 1876, the deficiency from the amount of the liabilities of the Government, and the value of the securities held by the Commissioners for the Reduction of the National Debt, amounted to £4,521,727

They prefer becoming *rentières,* or fundholders, to having money at their disposal at the savings bank, and still more they like a plot of ground which they may call their own. The subdivision of land in France certainly favours this, and the Frenchman delights in it. In England land is not to be had. The funds do not present much facility for investment. Whilst in England no more than 228,696 persons are entitled to various amounts of dividends on the several kinds of stock in the public funds, in France the number of fundholders is given at 5,500,000. It is safety and physical grasp of the property that mostly attract the Frenchman. The Englishman is quite prepared to hazard a little more for profit. After all, the savings banks offer no sufficient compensation. All they do is to keep for you any sum of money you please, paying you as high a rate of interest as, and indeed more than, money is worth in this great storehouse of capital.

Next to having some ready money always available in case of need, we do well if we can make provision to secure some help in case of sickness, or special contingencies; and here come to our aid the many friendly societies. In the savings banks the depositor's capital remains his own, he has full freedom to use it howsoever he likes, and can withdraw it whenever he likes. In a friendly society the capital of the members constitutes a common fund; the investor is understood to devote the amount to the object of the society, and he can get the fund back only on the happening of certain events. The purposes of friendly societies are very varied. They relieve members in sickness and old age; they furnish proper medicine and medical attendance; they provide members with assistance when travelling in search of employment; they assist them when in distress; they provide a sum on the death of members for their widows and children; and they defray the expense of burial. A complete list of such societies in every part of the kingdom would show how extensively the spirit of association is in operation. First is the Manchester Unity of Odd Fellows. Next is the Ancient Order of Foresters, marching under the banner of " Every man for every man, himself included." The Rechabite Temperance Friendly Society has for its motto, " We will drink no wine, for Jonadab the son of Rechab our father commanded us saying, Ye shall drink no wine, neither ye nor your sons, for ever." Besides these, and among many others, we have the " Royal Standard," " Hearts of Oak Benefit Society," " The Order of Druids," " The Loyal Order of Ancient Shepherds," " The Order of the Golden Fleece," " The Star of the East," and many more, numbering together one million and a quarter of members. After these come the burial societies, with another million and half of members. Then the societies of women, such as the " Odd Sisters," the " Comforting Sisters," the " United Sisters," and " The Daughters of Temperance." The Scottish Societies go by the names of " The Humane," " The Protector," " The Bon-Accord," " The Thistle." Ireland has her " Emerald Isle Tontine Society," the " Adam and Eve Tontine," the " St. Dominic," " St. Ignatius," " St. Joseph," and many more. Besides the friendly societies proper, there are the trade unions, which are friendly societies and something more ; the industrial and provident societies, constituted for carrying on trade ; the loan societies and co-operative societies, which have of late made wonderful progress. These friendly societies have been divided by the commissioners into seventeen classes. And even these by no means exhaust all the varieties of societies thus formed. Are they all solvent ? Can they be all recommended ? Their object is, doubtless, good, their intention excellent. But do they take proper precautions in their investments of money. Do they take sufficient account of the rate of mortality in the different employments. Are the returns they give reliable ? Should any society of this character be allowed to meet at public-houses ? I do hope the Act recently passed may eventually afford sufficient guarantees for the 4,000,000 members interested in such societies, having together about £10,000,000 or £12,000,000, who, after all, are at the mercy of their committees. But what can the law do to protect private individuals from blunders, over-confidence, or positive rashness? By all means connect yourselves with such societies, but prefer certainly those which are registered, those whose accounts are properly audited, and those which can produce real certificates that they are sound, solvent, and safe.*

Of all friendly societies the most useful, when properly used, are the building societies; and these are either terminating or permanent. A terminating society is one whose members subscribe certain monthly or periodical sums, which accumulate till the funds are sufficient to give a stipulated sum to each member, when the whole is divided amongst them. The members of such societies may have the amount of their share in anticipation, by allowing a large discount,—not all, however, but such as, by a sort of auction, bid the highest sum of discount, the repayment being secured by mortgages on real or household property. The permanent societies do not dissolve upon the completion of the shares. In a terminating society a person must either become a member at the time the society is established or else pay a large amount of back subscriptions. In a permanent, one may become a member at any time. In a terminating, one does not know how long he has to continue his payments, and how much he may withdraw. In a permanent, he does. Together they have a capital of some £12,000,000, of which perhaps £8,000,000 may belong to the working classes. Are building societies advantageous as an investment for the working classes? Are they safe? Properly conducted, a building society ought to be safe,

---

* It has been proposed that the Government should establish a National Friendly Society, in connection with the Post Office Savings Banks; but the fatal objections to such a scheme are the absence of any reliable data of the causes and duration of sickness, the great liability to deception, the cost of management, and the difficulty of securing the continuance of payments.

for it invests its funds in houses and other real property, and it ought to be able to calculate exactly what its funds at compound interest are likely to produce. And as for convenience, I can conceive no investment more attractive than one which may enable you in a comparatively few years to have a house of your own. In London, indeed, the distance between your house and your work, the expense of living in the suburbs, and the uncertainty of remaining long in any employment in any locality, may prove an obstacle to the purchase of a house, but I cannot conceive a more mischievous disposition in any family than that of being continually shifting from place to place. "A rolling stone gathers no moss." What waste is the expense of removing! What unfixedness of habits! What discouragement to beautify your house—to make it a home. Stay still, my friends. And by all means if you can, buy a house for yourselves. It is the best and most profitable expenditure you can possibly make.

The building society will provide you with a house to dwell in. The friendly society will see that in sickness you have a doctor, and that on your death you may have a decent burial. But what of the friends you must leave behind? For any security to them, you must have recourse to the provident principle of life insurance. Based on the fixedness of the law of nature, which not only lays a bound to our natural life, but seems to indicate what proportion of any given number of human beings is likely to die, at every age, the life insurer is ready to take upon himself the obligation to pay a certain amount to your friends and relatives whenever you may die, be it to-morrow or fifty years hence, provided you engage to pay, and do actually pay, every year, as long as you live, a fixed annual premium. Suppose you have a wife and children, and you are anxious that when you die they shall not remain penniless. If you are thirty years of age you will have to pay, say, £2 1s. 6d. per annum to secure £100 at death for your friends.

But mind you—and this is a hard measure in life insurance—that if you do miss a single year, you lose all you have put in. After, say, ten years, you may surrender the policy to the Office, and get some allowance for what you have paid. But not before. But can workmen engage to make annual payments, and can they be sure of continuing them? This is indeed the difficulty, for the collection of weekly payments is very costly, and hitherto, where insurance has been tried among working men, the proportion of lapses is very large. It is certainly an advantage, in life insurance, that it compels you to make some self-sacrifice, nay, to make a very hard struggle every year, somehow, to pay the premium; for the longer you pay it the safer is the policy. You are not likely to grudge paying the premium, because you wish for yourself length of days, whatever it may cost. And the insurance company will be glad if you live very long, if you become a very centenarian, for then it will get the premium out of you twice or three times over. But workmen having uncertain employments have great difficulty to meet the demands of life insurance. Nevertheless, I do wish life insurance could be extended among the labouring classes, for it is of great comfort and benefit, and the upper and middle classes use it largely, upwards of £300,000,000 being insured upon their lives, upon which they pay more than £10,000,000 per annum in premium. The Government has provided for the granting of Government annuities and insurance in connection with the Post Office; and there if you only succeed in paying the premium for five years, you will be entitled, if you wish to discontinue it, to the surrender value. But the working classes do not seem to have taken much advantage of the plan. Founded as far back as 1865, contracts have been entered into for the purpose by the Post Office, for less than £300,000. Insurance companies do not come to you. You must go to them. If you do decide upon insuring, take care to choose the safest office; for valuable as life insurance is, it should not be forgotten that the actual solvency of the company depends on the accuracy of the data upon which it carries on its business, on the rate of mortality which they assume, on the rate of interest which they are able to realize, and on the portion of income from premium which they are able to reserve for future expenses and profits. In the words of Messrs. Malcolm and Hamilton, who have reported on the accounts of insurance companies, "taking insurance business as it exists in this country, where adequate premiums are charged, and lives selected with care, the public cannot be misled if, when seeking an office in which to effect an insurance, they select one which transacts its business at a small percentage of working cost, and does not anticipate its profits."

I have mentioned among the friendly societies the co-operative societies, both for distribution and production. Co-operative societies may be regarded as a means of investment, and as a mode of securing a more liberal reward for labour. It is not indeed put forth that either co-operative societies or industrial partnerships can supersede effectually, or in any important degree, the present relation of capital and labour, as by far the simplest and capable of the widest application, yet it is conceived that by affording greater encouragement to save, and ampler opportunities for the profitable use of such savings, many who at present have no other prospect than that of remaining in a condition of comparative dependence, may eventually become possessed of a small capital. How to give to the consumer direct access to the producer; how to give to the immediate producer, that is, labour, direct access to capital, either directly, by an antecedent act of aggregate saving on the part of the producer himself, or mediately, by crediting the immediate producer or labourer with the necessary capital,—these are the objects which co-operation seeks to obtain. Co-operative societies have been formed for distribution and production, and even for credit. The conception is certainly simple and practical. Here are a hundred men, consuming yearly, say, £40 each, at least, of commodities, which if bought wholesale will cost no more than £30. Form a co-operative society to buy direct such provisions from the producer, and the profit which the retailers would have gained will form a substantial economy to the consumers. Or let the price of the commodities consumed remain as they would be if sold by retailers, and let the profits accumulate in the hands of such society; and you will have, by degree, a handsome capital belonging to such members, which may be employed in production. And thus, from a co-operative society for distribution, you may easily rise to a co-operative society for production. Here are a thousand operatives, each having a small saving. Gather their savings together to form the capital. Let the contributors be themselves the operatives, and the combination will seem perfect. But how should the relative rights of capital and labour be adjusted? The workman, as a capitalist, has an interest in increasing, as much as possible, the profits of the establishment, but as a workman he is still more interested in securing a liberal rate of wages. Here an antagonism of interests is sure to follow, and it is a great question whether the problem admits of a satisfactory solution. But I have supposed the existence of capital in the hands of the labourers. What if they have no such capital? Can they be credited with it? What security can they offer? Shall we ask the State to lend capital to such labourers if the capitalists will not incur the risk? The idea is in itself preposterous.

Take, however, the most probable case, where labourers have only a very small capital. Shall we encourage them to employ their savings in co-operative societies for production? A large portion of the success which attends commercial operations is the result of the skill and shrewdness of those who engage in them. Capital is an important element, but the capacity to know when and where to buy and to sell, and the possession of a spirit of adventure balanced by prudence and caution, are elements of enormous value in securing success. Can working men lay claim to such knowledge and foresight? If they have to depend upon others for the management of such undertakings, is there no danger of their falling into the hands of designers and schemers, who will soon squander the little savings? Of the many industrial co-operative societies formed for productive purposes, but very few have at all succeeded. Looking over the returns of such societies, I find that whilst such as are for distribution—as grocers, drapers, and provision dealers—have succeeded exceedingly well, scarcely any formed for productive purposes can show any real gain. Whilst the Rochdale Equitable Pioneers—as grocers, provision dealers, drapers, tailors—realized a goodly sum, the Rochdale card manufacture realized nothing, and so in a number of instances. The recent abandonment of the principle of industrial partnership by Messrs. Briggs has been exceedingly disappointing to the friends of co-operation; and so also has the breakdown of the Ouseburn Engine Works, of the Shirland Colliery, and the Industrial Bank in Newcastle. To my mind, there is no royal road to wealth. The workman must, in some measure, become a capitalist himself before he can seek to become a co-operator with the capitalist in industrial enterprise. And when he has amassed a little sum, let him take care what he does with it. In these days, production on a small scale has no chance of success in competition with production on a large scale. Great enterprises, with large capital, are carried on at much less expense, and can always command greater facilities. Lay you a solid foundation for your advancement in a substratum of real capital, foster it by prudence and foresight, increase it by legitimate means, and you may depend upon it that in *that* you will have the surest safeguard for independence and improvement.

The introduction of limited liability in joint stock companies has opened for the working classes the avenues to commercial operations to any extent. All you require is capital, and this capital you must gather, little by little, by hard labour, and, it may be, by continuous toil and hardship. Gentlemen, it requires some amount of heroism to set aside any fragment of our present income for our future wants, to deprive ourselves, it may be, of needed comforts that we may provide for contingencies at present, at least, beyond our ken. But it is worth doing. A pound to-day and another to-morrow. Now five pounds and anon ten—it is astonishing how soon the sum grows, if you are only careful. But be you extra cautious how you invest your savings, for the more labour we have to give to the acquisition of small incomes and the accumulation of small savings, the more incumbent it becomes on us to be on our guard, lest we should lose it all by carelessness or misemployment. Trust not on the Government to protect you. Keep your eyes open, and mind what you are about, for once you lose what you have got, it is extremely difficult to get it again. After all, it is not much we want. Strive for more, but be content with your lot.

> "Man's rich with little, were his judgments true;
> Nature is frugal, and her wants are few:
> Those few wants answer'd, bring sincere delights;
> But fools create themselves new appetites."

But, my friends, is it only money that we should seek after? Are there not treasures of knowledge, treasures of benefaction, treasures of inward joys and happiness, that we may aspire to obtain? Must we all strike the same path? Have we all the same talents? Have we all the same opportunities? Thirty-two years ago, a comparative youth came to England, from the centre of Italy, unknowing and unknown. He had but one talent—not that of the Universities, either of Oxford or Cambridge, Pisa or Bologna; not that of riches, or of fame; but one common to all—an open eye and an open mind, with perseverance in duty, and hope and faith to cheer him in his path. He planted that talent in the British soil, and there it lodged summer and winter, and winter and summer, giving little signs of life; but it was growing, and it gave fruit in the establishment of a Chamber of Commerce in Liverpool, in a work on the Commercial Law of the World, and another on the History of British Commerce. And that talent is still growing, and has made its possessor a barrister-at-law, a member of not a few scientific societies, and the Professor of the Principles of Commerce and Commercial Law in King's College, London;—the very one who has now the honour and the pleasure of addressing to you these Lectures. If you could trace the antecedents of many of those who are now great, how often would you find that it is not fortune, or birth, or estate, that produces our best men, but labour, perseverance, force of will. Read Smiles' "Self-made Men;" and you will find that Hargreaves and Crompton were artizans, and Arkwright a barber. That Telford and Hugh Miller were stonemasons, and Trevithick a mechanic. That Lord Tenterden the judge, and Turner the painter, were both sons of barbers. That Inigo Jones the architect, and Hunter who discovered the circulation of the blood, were carpenters. That Cardinal Wolsey and Defoe were sons of butchers; that the immortal John Bunyan was a tinker, and Herschel the astronomer a bandsman. That James Watt was the son of an instrument maker, and Faraday the son of a blacksmith; that Newton's father was a yeoman, with a small farm worth $11s.\ 6\frac{1}{2}d.$ a year; and Milton the son of a scrivener. That Pope and Southey were sons of linendrapers, and Shakspeare the son of a butcher and grazier. That Lord Eldon was the son of a Newcastle coalfitter, and Lord St. Leonard the son of a barber, who began life as an errand boy. All honour to them! Strive you to be like them.

> "Lives of great men all remind us,
> We can make our lives sublime,
> And, departing, leave behind us
> Footprints on the sands of time;

> Footprints, that perhaps another,
>   Sailing o'er life's solemn main,
> A forlorn and shipwrecked brother,
>   Seeing, shall take heart again.
>
> Let us, then, be up and doing,
>   With a heart for any fate;
> Still achieving, still pursuing,
>   Learn to labour and to wait."

Let our occupation be high or low in public estimation, he is a great man who, by high character and self-mastery, by culture and industry, by application and perseverance, secures for himself a true individuality; and who, with powers fully developed, and faculties duly expanded, uses whatever talent he may possess to the glory of God, and to the benefit of his fellow-creatures.

APPENDIX A.

Statement of the weekly expenditure, in 1859, of a family consisting of husband, wife, and three children, whose total wages averaged thirty shillings per week, as compared with the cost of the same articles in 1875, 1849, and 1839.—"Progress of Manchester," by D. Chadwick, British Association, 1861, revised by Dr. Watts.

Articles.	Expenditure in 1875.			Expenditure in 1859.			Expenditure in 1849.			Expenditure in 1839.		
		s.	d.		s.	d.		s.	d.		s.	d.
(I.) Bread, Flour, and Meal.												
3 4lb. loaves (32 lbs.)	6½d. per 4lbs.	4	4	5½d. per 4lb.	3	8	6d. per 4lbs.	4	0	8½d. per 4lb.	5	8
½ a peck of meal	1s. 10d. pr. pk.	0	11	1s. 8d. per pk.	0	10	1s. 6d. per pk.	0	9	1s. 4d. per pk.	0	8
½ a doz. (6 lbs.) of flour	1s. 10d. pr. dz.	0	11	1s. 8d. per dz.	0	10	1s. 10d. pr. dz.	0	11	2s. 4d. per dz.	1	2
		6	2		5	4		5	8		7	6
(II.) Butchers' Meat and Bacon.												
5lbs. of butchers' meat	8½d. per lb.	3	6½	6½d. per lb.	2	8½	7d. per lb.	2	11	6½d. per lb.	2	8½
2lbs. of bacon	9d. "	1	6	3d. "	1	4	3d. "	1	6	3d. "	1	4
		5	0½		4	0½		4	5		4	0½
(III.) Potatoes, Milk, and Vegetables.												
2 score of potatoes	1s. per score	2	0	1s. per score	2	0	1s. per score	2	0	1s. per score	2	0
7 quarts of milk	4d. per qt.	2	4	3d. per qt.	1	9	3d. per qt.	1	9	3d. per qt.	1	9
Vegetables	....	0	6	....	0	6	....	0	6	....	0	6
		4	10		4	3		4	3		4	3
(IV.) Groceries, Coals, etc.												
½lb. of coffee	1s. 4d. per lb.	0	8	1s. 4d. per lb.	0	8	1s. 4d. per lb.	0	8	2s. per lb.	1	0
¼lb. of tea	2s. 8d. "	0	8	4s. "	1	0	4s. 4d. "	1	1	6s. "	1	6
3lbs. of sugar	4d. "	1	0	5d. "	1	3	5d. "	1	3	7d. "	1	9
2lbs. of rice	2d. "	0	4	3d. "	0	6	3d. "	0	6	4d. "	0	8
1lb. butter	1s. 1d. "	1	1	1s. 1d. "	1	1	1s. "	1	0	1s. 1d. "	1	1
2lbs. of treacle	2½d. "	0	5	2½d. "	0	5	3d. "	0	6	4d. "	0	8
1½lbs. of soap	4d. "	0	6	4d. "	0	6	5d. "	0	7½	5d. "	0	7½
Coals	....	1	6	....	1	0	....	1	0	....	1	0
Candles	....	0	6	....	0	6	....	0	6	....	0	6
		6	8		6	11		7	1½		3	9½
Rent, taxes, and water	....	4	0	....	4	0	....	4	0	....	4	0
Clothing	....	3	0	....	3	0	....	3	0	....	3	0
Sundries	....	2	5½	....	2	5½	....	2	5½	....	2	5½
		9	5½		9	5½		9	5½		9	5½
Totals		32	2		30	0		30	11		34	0½

APPENDIX.

AVERAGE WEEKLY EARNINGS OF THE COTTON OPERATIVES.

	Week of 69 hours.		Week of 60 hours.	
	1839	1849	1859	1873
	s. d.	s. d.	s. d.	s. d.
Steam-engine tenders	24 0	28 0	30 0	32 0
Warehousemen	18 0	20 0	22 0	26 0
Carding stretchers	7 0	7 6	8 0	12 0
Strippers, young men, women, and girls	11 0	12 0	14 0	19 0
Overlookers	25 0	28 0	28 0	32 0
Spinners on self-acting Winders, Males	16 0	18 0	20 0	25 0
Piecers, women and young men	8 0	9 0	10 0	16 0
Overlookers	20 0	22 0	26 0	30 0
Reeling Throttle, reelers, women	9 0	9 6	9 6	12 6
Warpers	22 0	22 0	23 0	26 0
Sizers	23 0	23 0	25 0	30 0
Doubling, Doublers, women	7 0	7 6	9 0	12 6
Overlookers	24 0	25 0	28 0	32 0

	1860. Per week.	1872. Per week.
Agricultural—		
Devon	8s. to 12s.	9s. to 12s.
Somerset	12s. „ 14s.	13s. „ 20s.
Cheshire	15s.	16s. 6d.
Durham	15s. to 20s.	17s. to 20s.
	1855.	1876.
Builders—		
Masons	5s. per day.	9d. per hour.
	1850. Per month.	1874. Per month.
Seamen, London—		
Mediterranean	45s.	70s. to 80s. ... 80s. to 90s.
North America	50s.	80s. „ 95s. ... 85s. „ 95s.
East India and China	40s.	60s. „ 65s. ... 80s. „ 85s
Australia	40s.	70s.

APPENDIX B.

BUDGETS OF THE WORKING CLASSES.

GREAT BRITAIN.
(From the "Times," November 19th, 1872.)

Weekly Expenses of a Farm Labourer in 1872 in East Sussex:—

	£ s. d.	Per week. £ s. d.
7 gallons of flour	0 7 0	
1 lb. butter	0 1 4	
2 oz. tea*	0 0 4	
2 lb. sugar*	0 0 7	
2 lb. cheese	0 1 3	
Milk	0 0 3½	
½ lb. soap	0 0 2	
Soda and blue	0 0 1	
1½ lb. candles	0 0 10½	
Schooling	0 0 7	
Cotton and mustard	0 0 3	
Washing and mangling	0 1 0	
Rent	0 2 0	
		0 15 10

Extra expenses per annum:—

	£ s. d.		
Benefit club	1 4 4		
Boots	2 14 0		
Clothes	1 0 0		
Tools	0 4 0		
Faggots	2 0 0		
Extra food in hop drying	0 10 0		
	7 12 4	equal to	0 3 0
			0 18 10

Income and Expenditure of a Tobacco Spinner in Edinburgh, the Family consisting of Six Persons. Income: Father, 25s.; Boy in the Telegraph Service, 6s.—total, 31s.

Expenditure :—

	£	s.	d.	Per cent.	Taxes.
Bread, 36lb.; meat, 4½lb.; flour, 7lb.; rice, 1lb.; potatoes, 10½ lb; sugar,* 5lb; tea,* ¼lb.; coffee,* ½lb.; butter, 1½lb.	0	16	6	54	0 6
Beer,* 4 pints; spirits *nil*; tobacco,* 3oz.	0	2	0	6	1 9
House rent	0	2	4	7	
Coal and gas	0	1	8	6	
Clothing	0	4	0	13	
Taxes	0	0	3½	1	0 3½
Church or chapel, 4d.; amusements, 1d.; benefit club, 1s. 1d.; doctor's bill, and sundries, 2s. 6d.	0	4	0	13	
	£1	10	9½	100	2 6½

Income and Expenditure of a Printer, Single Man, living in London. Income £1 16s. 0d. a-week :—

	£	s.	d.	Per cent.	Taxes.
Bread, 12lb.; meat, 4lb.; flour, 4lb.; potatoes, 8lb.; sugar,* 1lb.; tea,* 2oz.; coffee,* 2oz.; butter, 10oz.	0	9	8	41	0 3
Beer,* 14 pints; spirits,* 1 quartern; tobacco,* 4oz.	0	5	0	21	1 4
House rent	0	2	6	11	
Coal and gas	0	1	6	6	
Clothin	0	2	6	11	
Church, amusements, laundress	0	2	6	10	
	£1	3	8	100	1 7

FRANCE.

(From Lord Brabazon's Report, 1872, p. 45.)

Average Expenditure of a Married Day Labourer's Family, consisting of Father, Mother, and Three Children, with a Collective Income of £24 1s. 7d.

	£	s.	d.	Per cent.
Bread,* vegetables, meat,* milk, salt	13	15	7	59
Wine,* beer,* and cider*	1	7	2	6
Lodging* (tax on doors and windows)	1	13	7	7
Firing*	1	5	8	5
Taxes	0	4	6	1
Clothing*	3	12	9	16
Other expenses	1	5	9	6
	£23	5	0	100

PRUSSIA.

(Dr. Engel's Table.)

Percentage of the Expenditure of the Family of

	A Working Man with an income of from £45 to £60 a year. Per cent.	A Man of Middle Class with an income from £90 to £120 a year. Per cent.	A Person in easy circumstances with an income from £150 to £220 a year. Per cent.
Subsistence	62	55	50
Clothing	16	18	18
Lodging	12	12	12
Firing and lighting	5	5	5
Education, public worship	2	3.5	5.5
Legal protection	1	2	3
Care of Health	1	2	3
Comfort, mental and bodily recreation	1	1.5	3.5
	100	100	100

NETHERLANDS.

(*Mr. Locock's Report*, 1871, p. 351.)

Weekly Expenses of a Mason, with a Wife and Two Children:—

	s.	d.		Per cent.
Bread,* butter, milk, sugar,* coffee,* suet, flour, potatoes, greens, meal, salt, bacon, oil, tobacco,* soap,* etc.	11	11	.	53
House rent	2	0	.	9
Firing*	1	3	.	6
Clothing*	2	1	.	9
Sundries	5	3	.	23
	22	6	.	100

SWITZERLAND (BALE).

(*M. Gould's Report*, 1872, p. 366.)

Yearly Expenditure of a Working Man's Family:—

	£	s.	d.		Per cent.
Bread, coffee, chicory, milk, potatoes, butter, oil, meat, vegetables	29	6	2	.	57
Rent	10	8	0	.	20
Wood	4	0	0	.	8
Taxes	0	6	5	.	0
Clothing	6	0	0	.	12
Sick Fund	0	16	0	.	3
	50	16	7	.	100

RUSSIA.

Annual Expenditure of a Peasant Family, consisting of Father and Son, Two Brothers, and a Third Young Man, in the Province of Novgorod:—

(*Consul Michel's Report on Land Tenure*, p. 63.)

	£	s.	d.
80¾ bush. rye from the land, 36lb. fish, 1 sack wheat, 2.88 bush. buckwheat, salt	3	0	0
Dress,* boots, etc.	2	13	4
Taxes, Imperial and Provincial, at 3 roubles per male	1	4	0
Village priest	0	2	8
	£7	0	0

APPENDIX.

(Consul Gregnon's Report, 1871, p. 54.)

Estimated Expenditure for a Single Man, Factory Hand, for a Day's Living in Riga :—

	d.
3 lbs. Russ. rye bread, at 2½ copecks	2¾
1 lb. Russ. meat	3⅜
Coffee,* sugar, and milk	1½
Potatoes	0½
Butter	0⅘
Herrings	0⅘
Barley meal	0⅘
	10

To the above must be added lodging, capitation-tax, clothing, and personal expenses.

(Consul Campbell's Report, 1872, p. 312.)

A Manufactory Workman's Monthly Expenditure at Helsingfors :—

		£	s.	d.		£	s.	d.
Food,	24 to 30 marks	0	19	0	to	1	3	9
Fuel,	2 „ 2½ „	0	1	7	„	0	2	0
Lodging,	10 „ 12 „	0	8	0	„	0	9	6
Clothing,*	10 „ 12½ „	0	7	0	„	0	9	6
		1	15	7		2	4	9

UNITED STATES (PENNSYLVANIA).

(Mr. Consul Kortright's Report, 1871, p. 921.)

Weekly Cost of Living of Two Parents and Three Children in Philadelphia :—

	£	s.	d.	Per cent.
Bread, flour, meat, butter, cheese, sugar,* milk, coffee,* tea,* fish, salt, eggs, potatoes, fruit	1	8	6	54
Rent	0	13	0	24
Light * and Fire	0	3	3	6
Clothing *	0	7	5	14
Taxes	0	0	4½	2
Other Expenses	0	0	9½	
	2	13	3	100

UNITED STATES.

(From the Sixth Annual Report of the Bureau of the Statistics of Labour.)

Percentage of the Expenditure of the Family of a Working Man with an income—

	From £60 to £90. Per cent.	£90 to £120. Per cent.	£120 to £150. Per cent.	£150 to £250. Per cent.	Above £250. Per cent.	Average Per cent.
Subsistence	64	63	60	56	51	58
Clothing	7	10·5	14	15	19	14
Rent	20	15·5	14	17	15	16
Fuel	6	6	6	6	5	6
Sundry Expenses	3	5	6	6	10	6
	100	100	100	100	100	100

APPENDIX C.

REPORT *of the Committee of the British Association for the Advancement of Science, on Combinations of Capital and Labour.* Lord Houghton, D.C.L., F.R.S. (chairman); Jacob Behrens, Esq.; Thomas Brassey, Esq., M.P.; Frank P. Fellows, Esq.; Archibald Hamilton, Esq.; Professor Leone Levi; A. J. Mundella, Esq., M.P.; Wm. Newmarch, Esq., F.R.S.; Lord O'Hagan; R. J. Inglis Palgrave, Esq.; Professor Thorold Rogers. Submitted by Professor Leone Levi, and ordered to be printed and laid before the Association.

YOUR Committee appointed to inquire into the economic effects of Combinations of labourers or capitalists, and into the laws of Economic science bearing on the principles on which such Combinations are founded, have already stated in their preliminary Report made last year, the course they have thought fit to take in order to ascertain the exact views held by both employers and employed on the subject in question. Although the general objects of such Combinations, whether of capitalists or labourers, are well known, both from the written rules which bind them together, and from the action taken from time to time, your Committee have deemed it desirable to come into personal contact with some representative men from both classes, with a view of finding whether they do now stand by the rules of their Unions, and how far they are prepared to defend them. And for that purpose, your Committee resolved to hold a consultative private conference of employers and employed in the presence of the members of the Committee, where they might discuss the questions involved in the resolution of the British Association, and with a view of reporting thereon to the same. The points more especially inquired into were the following :—

1st. What determines the minimum rate of wages?

2nd. Can that minimum rate be uniform in any trade, and can that uniformity be enforced?

3rd. Is Combination capable of affecting the rate of wages, whether in favour of employers or employed?

4th. Can an artificial restriction of labour or of capital be economically right or beneficial under any circumstances?

For the discussion of these questions your Committee had the advantage of bringing together a deputation from the National Federation of Associated Employers of Labour, including Messrs. R. R. Jackson, M. A. Brown, H. R. Greg, Joseph Simpson, J. A. Marshall, R. Hannen, and Henry Whitworth. As representing labour : Messrs. Henry Broadhurst, Daniel Guile, George Howell, Loyd Jones, George Potter, and Robert Newton ; Mr. Macdonald, M.P., and Mr. Burt, M.P., having been prevented from attending. And on the part of your Committee there were Lord Houghton, Professor Rogers, Mr. Samuel Brown, Mr. W. A. Hamilton, Mr. Frank Fellows, and Professor Leone Levi.

Many are the works and documents bearing on the questions at issue. Of an official character we have the Report of the Royal Commission appointed " to inquire into and report upon he organization and rules of Trade Unions and other associations, whether of workmen and employers and to inquire into and report on the effects produced by such Trade Unions and associations on the workmen and employers and on the relations between workmen and employers and on the trade and industry of the country." Of an unofficial character we have the Report of the Committee of the Social Science Association "on the objects and constitution of Trade Societies, with their effects upon wages and upon the industry and commerce of the country." Of special works we have the late lamented Professor Cairnes' "Leading Principles of Political Economy," Mr. Thomas Brassey's "Work and Wages," and Professor Leone Levi's "Wages and Earnings of the Working Classes."

The chief functions of Combinations, whether of Capital or Labour, being to operate on wages, your Committee were anxious to ascertain by what criterion the parties interested ordinarily judge of the sufficiency or insufficiency of existing wages. The first test of the sufficiency of wages is the relation they bear to the cost of the necessaries of life. "The minimum of wages," said Prof. Rogers, " is the barest possible amount upon which a workman can be maintained ; that which, under the most unfavourable circumstances, a man is able to obtain." But the minimum thus estimated can only be, and is, submitted to under circumstances of extreme necessity. " I believe the minimum rate of wages," said one of the representatives of labour, " is that which, under the worst circumstances, the worst workman gets from the worst master." We cannot, therefore, take the minimum rates so considered as a proper basis for the sufficiency of wages. How far insufficient wages in relation to the cost of living in the United Kingdom is a cause of the large emigration which is taking place from year to year it is not possible to establish;* but, doubtless, the prospect held out in the distant Colonies and in the United States of America of considerable improvement has been for some time past and still is a strong inducement to those in receipt of insufficient wages in this country to emigrate to other lands. Your Committee are desirous to point out in connection with this question that not only has the cost of some of the principal necessaries of life greatly risen within the last twenty years, but that in consequence of the general increase of comfort and luxury many articles of food, drink, and dress must now be counted as necessaries which some years ago were far beyond the reach of the labouring classes; whilst house rent, especially adapted for the labouring classes, is considerably dearer. If, therefore, the cost of living be taken as a guide to the rate of wages, it would not be enough to take into account the cost of the mere necessaries of life. A higher standard of living having been established, it would be indispensable to compare the wages of labour to such higher standard. Your Committee are not satisfied, however, that it is possible to regulate wages according to the scale of comfort or luxury which may be introduced among the people, and are compelled to assert that it is an utter fallacy to imagine that wages will rise or fall in relation to the cost which such supposed necessaries or indulgences may entail.

A better test of the sufficiency of wages is the relation they bear to the state of the labour market; and tested by that standard the minimum rate of wages which workmen are at any time prepared to accept is the least which they think they are entitled to have under existing circumstances, the Trade Unions guiding them as to the state of trade and the value of labour at the time. Unfortunately, however, what workmen think themselves entitled to have does not always correspond with what employers find themselves able to grant. Primarily, the wages of labour are determined by the amount of capital available for the purpose of wages in relation to the number of labourers competing for the same. But the amount of capital employed in any industry is itself governed by considerations of the relation of the cost of production to the market price of the produce—that is, to the price which the consumer is able or willing to give for the same: the cost of production including the cost of materials, the value of capital, the cost of superintendence, and the wages of labour.

* The average number of emigrants in the last ten years from the United Kingdom, from 1862 to 1873, was 239,000 per annum. In 1873, the total number was 310,612, and in 1874, 241,014. The emigration to the United States decreased from 233,073 in 1873, to 148,161 in 1874.

Objection has been taken at the Conference to this method for arriving at the rate of wages; and it was urged that instead of taking the price of the article produced, or the interest of the consumer, as the basis of the calculation, the first ingredient in the cost of the article should be the price to be paid to the workman in producing it. But a serious consideration will show that the employer cannot ignore what the consumer can or will pay any more than the share which the value of capital, the cost of superintendence, and the cost of the materials have upon the cost of production; for he must cease producing altogether if he cannot both meet the ability of the consumer to purchase his article and successfully compete with the producers of other countries. Your Committee think that it is not in the power of the employer to control the proportion of the different elements in the cost of production, each of them being governed by circumstances peculiar to itself. The value of Capital, as well as the value of the raw materials, is regulated by the law of supply and demand, not only in this country, but in the principal markets of the world. The cost of superintendence and the wages of labour are likewise governed by the relation of the amount of capital to the number seeking to share in the different employments. The employed say, "We must have certain wages. We care for nothing else. Labour is our property. We set our value upon it. If you will have our labour you must pay what we ask for it. And if such wages should require a rise in the market price, let the consumer pay it." What however, if the consumer will not or cannot pay sufficient price to enable the employer to pay such wages? What, if he can get the article cheaper elsewhere? Must not production cease if there be no market? And where will be the wages if there be no production? Nor should it be forgotten that a general rise of wages producing an increase of the cost of all the commodities of life reacts on the masses of the people, and thus far neutralizes the benefit of higher wages.

Disagreements between employers and employed are often produced on the subject of wages by the fact that all the elements of the case are not within the cognizance of both parties; experience showing that in making a demand for an advance of wages, or for resisting a fall, workmen are of necessity groping in the dark as to the real circumstances of the case. One of the chief advantages supposed to result from the organization of Trade Unions is the competency of their leaders to give solid and practical advice to those interested, as to the condition of the labour market; and we have no doubt that this duty is in the main honestly performed, but it is very much to expect that such leaders should universally possess large and liberal views enough to vindicate the exercise of their enormous power, and such constant and accurate knowledge of the multiple facts of the case as would enable them to exercise an almost infallible authority. On the other hand, were it possible for employers, who are not in the dark in such matters, to make known to their own workmen the grounds of the action they propose taking before the resolve is carried into execution, your Committee are convinced that many disputes would be avoided, and much of the jealousy which now exists between the parties would be removed. The recent lock-out in South Wales illustrated the need of such a course. Had the facts which Lord Aberdare elicited from the principal colliery firms in Glamorganshire been made known previous to or simultaneously with the notice of a fall, it is a question whether such a widespread calamity would have occurred. It is perhaps a natural but unfortunate circumstance that employers are seldom found to take the initiative in allowing a rise in wages when the state of the market permits it as they are in case of a fall, and spontaneously to offer what they must sooner or later be compelled to grant. A more prompt and politic course on their part in this matter would go far to neutralise the hostile action of Trade Unions.

Your Committee were anxious to ascertain how far is it in the mind of the employed that the employers obtain for themselves too large a share of profits at their expense. Your Committee were assured that no such doubts are entertained, though cases were produced supporting such suspicions by reference to the time of the great rise in the price of coals in 1873, when workmen's wages did not, in the opinion of the representatives of labour, rise to anything like the proportion of the masters' profits.* Your Committee admit that in cases of great oscillations in prices, the share participated either by the employers in the shape of profits, or by the employed in the shape of wages, may be for a time greater or less than their normal distribution would justify. And it is possible that some portions of these extra profits may be unproductively spent or so employed as not to benefit the parties more immediately concerned, and even used in totally alien speculations. Yet, in the main, the working classes must receive in one way or another, a considerable advantage from them, there being no doubt that the largest portion of such extra profits will be reinvested in the

* Mr. Halliday's evidence before the Committee of the House of Commons on coals, was that, though the custom was to give to workmen a portion of any rise of prices in the shape of increasing wages, the proportion being an additional 2*d.* a day for every 10*d.* a ton, the rise in wages was often 1*d.* per ton only and sometimes nothing, whilst when the price rose 2*s.* 6*d.* to 5*s.* a ton the wages were only increased 3*d.* a day.

ordinary industries of the country. In the end, however, wages and profits will be divided among the producers in proper proportions, and if at any time profits or wages should be larger than they ought to be, we may be quite sure that ere long the competition of capitalists will tend either to the lowering of prices or the raising of wages so as to make profits and wages gravitate towards each other.

Immediately allied to the question of the determination of a minimum of wages is that of their uniformity. In the opinion of many Trade Unions, all workmen of average ability in any trade should earn the same wages, the average ability of each man being understood to have been determined in advance by the fact of his being admitted as a member of the Union. But a man is subject to no examination, and is generally admitted upon the testimony of those who have worked with him, whose evidence must frequently be fallacious and insufficient. Nor does it appear that the rejection is absolutely certain even if the applicant should not be deemed a man of average ability, the acceptance or rejection of the party being always optional with the lodge to which he is introduced. Your Committee are therefore not satisfied that any guarantees exist that every member of a Union is able to earn a fair day's wages for a fair day's work; and they cannot, therefore, agree in the proposition that all workmen should be entitled to uniform wages on the ground of uniform ability. But another reason has been alleged for the uniformity of wages—which is still less tenable than the former—viz., a supposed uniformity of production independent of skill. The right of the workman to a uniform standard of wages was stated to be the production of an article which, though demanding less skill to perform, is of equal utility and is proportionally as profitable to the employer. Your Committee must, however, entirely demur to the principle that, in the apportionment of wages, no account should be taken of the skill brought to bear on the execution of the task, since a system of that nature would act as a premium on inferiority of workmanship. Again, by another test should the right of each individual to earn certain wages be determined, and that is by his productive capacity. Professor Levi asked whether that was taken into account when the workman was assumed to be of average ability; and the answer was that the amount of production depended largely upon the skill. "The more skilful a man is the more he will produce." But whilst, in so far as this answer was correct, it contradicted the principle embodied in the preceding test, the answer itself did not take sufficiently into account that skill is not the only element in effectiveness of labour. There are qualities of mind, judgment, and even of heart, disposition, and of moral character, which go far to increase or diminish the efficiency of labour ; and of such qualities the employer is, of necessity, a far better judge than any Union can be. That under ordinary circumstances wages in any trade should tend to uniformity is quite possible. The facility of communication and the extension of intercourse of necessity equalise prices and wages: but any attempt to compel uniformity of wages among any large number of men of varied capacity must of necessity prove a source of disappointment. Much, again, may be said in favour of a common standard of wages in any industry, as avoiding the embarrassment necessarily encountered in any attempt to adjust the rate to the exact worth of each individual. Yet it is impossible to ignore the fact that, whilst a uniform rate is sure to operate unjustly in favour of persons who may be wanting in fairness of dealing or capacity for workmanship, in the nature of things it is almost incapable to exist over a wide area, having regard to the varieties in the prices of fuel, carriage, house accommodation, or of the means of livelihood, as well as in the cost of raw materials and in the processes employed as affecting the rate of production of each individual. On the whole, your Committee find that an absolute uniformity in the rate of wages in any trade, though to a certain extent convenient, is neither just nor practicable, whilst any effort to compel uniformity in the amount of earnings of any number of individuals must prove fallacious and wrong as an illegitimate interference with the rights of industry.

A still more important question in connection with the subject is how far Combination of any kind can affect permanently or temporarily the rate of wages. Upon this, as might be expected, the most divergent opinions are held by the representatives of Capital and Labour. The employers of labour, standing on the solid principles of political economy, deny that Combinations can under any circumstances affect the rates of wages, at least in any permanent manner. The argument adduced being that if workmen are entitled to higher wages they are sure to get them, since, under the law of supply and demand, whenever it is found that profits trench unduly upon wages fresh capital is sure to be introduced, which provides for the raising of wages. The employed, on the other hand, confidently appeal to past experience, and point out the fact that almost every increase of wages has been due to the action of Trade Unions. They say that without Combination workmen cannot secure the market price for their labour, but are to a certain extent at the mercy of their employers. That in trades where one establishment employs a large number of workmen the employers can discharge a single workman with comparatively slight inconvenience, while the workman loses his whole means of subsistence. That without the machinery of Combination the workmen, being dependent upon their daily work for their daily bread, cannot hold on for a market.

Your Committee are not prepared to deny that Combinations can render useful service in matters of wages; but they think that it is impossible for them to frustrate or alter the operations of the laws of supply and demand, and thereby to affect permanently the rates of wages. Combination may hasten the action of those laws which would undoubtedly, though perhaps more slowly, operate their own results. The limited power of Combinations is in effect admitted by the workmen themselves. "We do not say," said one of the workmen's representatives, "that Trade Unions can absolutely interfere with supply and demand, because, when trade is very bad, they cannot obtain the standard; when it is good they easily raise the standard. What they do is, they enable workmen sooner to strike at the right time for a general advance. They get the advance sooner than if they were an undisciplined mob, having no common understanding. And when trade is receding, the common understanding enables workmen to resist the pressure put upon them by their employers. It helps them in both ways, and the workmen find they can act together beneficially." The ground here taken by the working-men is not at variance with sound economic principles. But there is yet another way in which Trade Unions may prove useful, and that is by rendering wages more sensitive to the action of the state of the market, and so preventing the influence of custom to stand in the way of the operation of supply and demand; for there are such occupations, as agriculture, where custom often exercises imperious rule even upon wages. As has been well said by M. Batbie, "Wages do not change unless the causes for the change exercise a strong influence. If the conditions of supply and demand do not undergo a great change, wages continue the same by the simple force of custom. The variations of wages are not like those of a thermometer, where the least clouds are marked, where one can read the smallest changes of temperature. They may rather be compared to those bodies which do not become heated except under the action of an elevated temperature, and remain quite insensible to the slight modifications of the atmosphere. Until a great perturbation takes place in the conditions of supply and demand, no one would think of changing the rate of wages."* After making every allowance your Committee cannot admit that Combinations have any power either to raise permanently the rate of wages or to prevent their fall when the conditions of trade require the same, as recent experience abun-

* See M. Batbie's article on "Salaries in Block's Dictionnaire de la Politique."

dantly shows, and, whilst admitting that Combinations may be beneficial in accelerating the action of economic laws, your Committee cannot be blind to the fact that they produce a state of irritation and discontent which often interferes with the progress of production.

Limited as is the power of Combinations to affect the rates of wages, still more limited is their power to affect materially the progress of productive industry. The Royal Commission on Trade Unions reported that it was extremely difficult to determine how far Unions have impeded the development of trade, whether by simply raising prices or by diverting trade from certain districts, or from this to foreign countries. The representatives of capital at the conference alluded to, endeavoured to prove that certain branches of trade have permanently been injured by the Unions. Whether the fact can be established or not, it is undeniable that British trade has enormously increased within the last twenty years, and that the exports of manufactured goods are on a larger scale now than they were at any former period.*

What is perhaps most objectionable in Combinations of labour is the method they often pursue in order to operate on the rates of wages; for they are not content with making a collective demand on employers for a rise, but endeavour to force it, or resist a fall, by restricting the supply of labour and increasing the need of it. One such method, explained at the Conference, seems to your Committee peculiarly objectionable. A representative of Labour said that when depression of trade comes, by means of associated funds the men are able to say to the surplus labourers, "Stand on one side—you are not wanted for the time being. If you go on with your labour at half-price, it will not mend the trade; we will not let you become a drug on the market, putting every other man down, but we will sustain you." In three years, your Committee were informed, over £100,000 was thus paid for unemployed labour, in the hope that undue fall in wages would be prevented by keeping labourers out of

---

* The following were the quantities of some of the principal articles of British produce and manufacture exported from the United Kingdom in 1854 and 1874:—

	1854	1874	Increase per cent.
Coal and Coke	tons 4,309,000	13,927,000	223
Copper	cwts. 274,000	709,000	159
Cotton Yarn	lbs. 147,128,000	220,599,000	49
Cotton Manufacture	yds. 1,692,899,000	3,606,639,000	113
Iron	tons 1,175,000	2,487,000	112
Worsted Manufacture	yds. 133,600,000	261,000,000	71

The total value of British produce exported increased from £135,891,000 in 1860 to £239,558,000 in 1874 or at the rate of 76 per cent.

the market. Your Committee are of opinion that the artificia prevention of a fall of wages when such a fall is necessary and inevitable, is economically wrong, and can only have the effect of still more injuring the condition of workmen, since by so doing they only throw hindrances in the way of production, which is the parent of all wages. Equally objectionable in your Committee's opinion, as interfering with the freedom of labour and with the general economy of production, is every regulation of such Trade Unions that excludes from employment in the trades all who have not been regularly apprenticed, or any rule which should set a limit to the number of apprentices. Professor Cairnes, commenting on the monopoly thus advocated by Trade Unions, said, " It is a monopoly, moreover, founded on no principle either of moral desert or of industrial efficiency, but simply on chance or arbitrary selection ; and which, therefore, cannot but exert a demoralizing influence on all who come within its scope—in all its aspects presenting an ungracious contrast to all that is best and most generous in the spirit of modern democracy."

The only other question on which your Committee will report is whether an artificial restriction of labour, or of capital, can under any circumstances be economically right or beneficial. It is, indeed, scarcely necessary to say that any restriction of Labour or of Capital, having the effect of limiting production, must of necessity prove injurious. Yet it may be a point for consideration whether under certain circumstances it may not be better for either Labour or Capital to submit to the evil of restriction in order to avoid a still greater evil, of producing at a loss, or working at rates of wages not sufficiently remunerative. The labourers justify their proceedings in this respect by reference to the practice of producers. One of the representatives of labour, speaking on this subject, said :—" No doubt there is not a working man in Lancashire who would not say that limitation was an injury. Generally that there should be the largest possible production in a given time is no doubt a true law, but every trade must regulate that according to its own necessities. The ironmaster blows out his furnaces when an increased production would injure; the cotton manufacturer runs his manufactory short time ; and the labourer limits the production." There is little or no difference in the relative position of Capital and Labour as respects their need of continuous production. Primarily, both employer and employed alike depend upon production as the only source for profits and wages. Whilst the employers have the maximun interest in producing as much as possible, from the fact that the fixed capital which they cannot withdraw would lie dormant and unproductive while the forge or mill is silent, the employed find it thier interest to aid in such production inasmuch as they depend upon it for their means of subsistence. The argument of the employed against a proposal for a reduction of wages is expressed in the words, "If you have too much of an article in the market and you cannot sell, I would rather limit the quantity in your hands than aggravate the evil and take less money for it." But by refusing to work when the employer is able or willing to continue producing, or by not submitting himself to accept lower wages when the inevitable law of supply and demand compels the same, the employed only aggravates his own position, whilst he places the employer in a still worse strait ; the certain consequence of the withdrawal of labour being to discourage production, to enhance the cost, and to increase the difficulty of foreign competition—injurious alike to the producer and to the whole community.

A frequent source of contention between employers and employed is the mode of paying wages—viz., by time, such as by the day or hour, or by piecework. There appears to be no uniform practice on the subject. While in some branches of industry the rule is to pay wages by piecework, in other branches the rule is to pay by time—the reason probably being that whilst in some branches it is easy to establish a scale of prices at which the work is to be paid for, in other branches such a scale could not easily be framed. In so far as the method of payment can be considered to affect production, it seems to your Committee that whilst payment by piecework is likely to promote quantity of production, payment by time is more likely to promote precision of execution. Your Committee cannot believe what has often been alleged, that payment by piecework is often offered to conceal any reduction of wages. If honestly acted upon on either side, payment by piecework has, in the opinion of your Committee, all the elements of fair justice. But the question in any case is not of sufficient importance to justify a breach of the friendly relation which should exist between Capital and Labour. When either party has any decided preference for one system, it seems advisable that the other party accept the same.

The economic effects of Strikes and Lock-outs are well known, and it matters but little which party in the contest in the end may prove successful. In recent years Strikes and Lock-outs have occurred among coal and iron miners, the building trade, engineers, the cotton trade, ship-builders, and most of the trades and industries of the country, each and all of which have caused serious losses on the community at large. In the opinion of your Committee a well-devised system of conciliation is the only proper and legitimate method of solving labour disputes. And your Committee cannot too strongly express their sense of the grave responsibility which rests on either employers or employed when, regardless of consequences, they resort to a step so vexatious and destructive as a strike or lock-out.

Your Committee are of opinion that the British Association will confer a lasting benefit if, on its pilgrimage in the principal industrial towns in the United Kingdom, it will seize every opportunity for the enunciation of sound lessons of political economy on the questions in agitation between employers and employed. It was suggested to your Committee that workmen should be admitted to the meetings of Section F at a reduced rate, and they commend the proposal to the consideration of the Council. Your Committee would also recommend to the Council to urge on Her Majesty's Government the importance of promoting, as far as possible, the study of political economy, and especially of those branches of industrial economy which most intimately concern the industry, manufactures, and commerce of the country. Your Committee have learned with pleasure that the Cobden Club are prepared to offer some encouragement for the teaching of political economy to the labouring classes, and your Committee would suggest that the Chambers of Commerce might advantageously take similar means in the great centres of commerce and manufacture. In the opinion of your Committee, a proper sense of the necessity and utility of continuous labour, an earnest desire for the achievement of excellence in workmanship in every branch of industry, and a keen and lively interest on the part of one and all to promote national prosperity, are the best safeguards against the continuance of those disturbances between Capital and Labour which have of late become of such hindrance to successful production. In the great contest which Britain has to wage with other industrial nations, it is the interest of both masters and men to be very careful, lest by raising the prices of British produce and manufacture too high they should no longer be able to carry the palm in the arena of international competition.

Your Committee regret the death of their much-esteemed member, Mr. Samuel Brown, who took an active part in the proceedings. Professor Fawcett, M.P., was unable to act. But your Committee have pleasure in reporting that the Right Hon. Lord O'Hagan, Mr. Thomas Brassey, M.P., and Mr. A. J. Mundella, M.P., were added to the Committee.

LEONE LEVI,
SECRETARY.

August, 1875.

INDEX.

AGRICULTURAL INDUSTRY, condition for progress of, 19
Arbitration *versus* Strikes, 94

BRITISH WORKMAN, characteristics of, 7
— productive power of, 8
Butter, consumption of, in 1844 and 1875, 11
Bacon, consumption of, in 1844 and 1875, 11
Building Societies, object of, 120
— permanent and terminating, 120

COMPETITION, foreign effects of machinery on, 32
Capital, production in England of, 33
— causes which arrested the growth of, 34
— difficulty of accumulating, 35
— obstacles to the diffusion of, 35
— what is? 36
— amount employed of, 41
— what determines the investment of, 41
— proportions of, distributed in production, 42
— stoppage of, accumulation of, 43
— consumption of, 44
— exportation of, 44
— abuse of, 46
— relation of, to labour, 49
— distribution of, between masters and men, 51
— and labour, partnership of, 51
Capitalists, how regarded, 68
Combinations, Old Laws on, 67
Co-operative Societies, for production and distribution, 123

Co-operative Societies, advantages of, 124

DAY'S WORK, what is it? 5
Division of labour, advantages of, 23
— disadvantages of, 24
Drunkenness, means of surmounting, 105
Drink, amount expended in, 109

EDUCATION, necessary for production, 12
— technical, advantages of, 13
England as a field of labour, 15
Employers' calculation of wages, 52
— duties towards employed, 54
— profits, 60
— risks of, 61
— power to amass wealth, 62
Earnings, of workmen, sources of, 99
— collective, what, 100
Expenditure of workmen, distribution of, 103
— economy in, 104
Earnings of workmen, total amount of, 108
Expenditure of workmen, total amount of, 108

FRENCH WORKMAN, characteristics of, 6
Food and drink, consumption of, in England, 11
— expenditure of workmen in, 104
Firing and lighting, expenditure of workmen in, 104
Friendly Societies, objects of, 118
— amount invested in, 119

GERMAN WORKMAN, characteristics of, 6

Health necessary for production, 8
Houses, healthiness of, 9
— high rents of, 9
Home, advantages of, 10
Home industry, condition of, 18
Hand loom and power loom, 18

ITALIAN WORKMAN, characteristics of, 7
Insurance (life), benefits of, 121
— amount insured, 122
— Government, 122

LABOUR, pleasures of, 1
— necessity of, 2
— value of, 3
— productive and unproductive, 3
— manual and mental, 4
— condition for the efficient discharge of, 5
— dangers attending, 8
— duration of, 12
— skilled and unskilled, 12
— division of, 22
— need of capital to, 37
— reward of, 49
— relation of, to capital, 49
— supply and demand of regulating, 57
— difficulties of, in contending wages with capital, 70
Lancashire, progress of, 19
Liverpool, increase of, 20
Labourers capitalists, 45

Morals an element in production, 14
Manufacture, divorcement of, from agriculture, 19
Manchester, increase of, 20
Machinery, advantages of, 25
— character of, 26
— effects of, 27
— relations of, to wages, 30, 61
— exports of, 31
Minimum wages, limits to, 85

Natural powers, utility of labour to, 37
Needlewomen, low wages of, 56

OVERTIME, action of Trade Unions on, 73

PAUPERISM, rate of, in 1849 and 1875, 11

Production on a large scale, advantages of, 22
— machinery of, 50
— requirements for, 52
— cost of, 52
Population, increase of, effect of, on wages, 57
Piecework, payment by, 78
Pay, what, 98
Poor Law, effects of, 100
— in Sweden, 101
— France, 101
— Belgium, 101
— Eberfeld, 101
Post Office Savings Banks, amount in, 114

SWISS WORKMAN, characteristic of, 7
Steam-power, advantages of, 21
Strikes and lock-outs, chances of, 85
— what, 86
— causes of, 86
— supposed advantages of, 87
— means to avoid, 88
— how promoted by Trade Unions, 90
— circumstances attending, 91
— effects of, 85
— cost of, 92
— losses caused by, 93
— arbitration or conciliation, versus, 94
Saving, duty of all respecting, 112
— first steps in, 112
Savings Banks, history of, 113
— amount invested in, 115
— post office and trustees, 116
— amount per head in England and Wales, 117
— Scotland, 117
— Ireland, 117
— France, 117
— Holland, 117
— Belgium, 117
— Austria, 117
— Germany, 117
— Switzerland, 117

TEA, consumption of, in 1844 and 1875, 11
Trade Unions, limits of usefulness of, 68
— limits of rights of, 69
— constitutional defects of, 70
— membership of, 71

INDEX.

Trades Unions, councils of, 71
— fees in, 72
— objects of, 72
— monopoly of, 72
— objection of, to overtime, 73
— operation of, on wages, 74
— effects of, on foreign competition, 82
— effects of, on the character of workmen, 83
— and benefit funds, 84
— rules of, respecting strikes, 88
Tobacco, expenditure of workmen in, 104
Taxation, effects of, on workmen, 108

WORKMEN, united labour and production of, 5
— difference of skill among, 5
Wheat and wheat flour, consumption of, in 1844 and 1875, 11
Wealth, benefits of, 46

Wages, what are, 51
— relation of, to profits, 53
Workman, interest of employer in, 54
Wages, lowering of, 54
— minimum rate of what, 55
— of artisans, 58
— what are the elements of, 58
— cost of, 58
Wage-fund, theory of, 60
Wages, effects of machinery on, 61
— uniformity of, 62, 71
— use of, 64
— effect of war on, 65
— attempt to regulate by law, 65
— effects of prohibition tariffs on, 65
— effects of Poor Law on, 65
— how affected by Trades Unions, 76
Working-classes, Budgets of, 96
Wages in money and in kind, 99
Workmen, taxes affecting, 107

www.ingramcontent.com/pod-product-compliance
Lightning Source LLC
Chambersburg PA
CBHW030314170426
43202CB00009B/1004